Retirement Planning for Couples

The Ultimate Financial Guide
to a Stress-Free and Happy Aging

Phoenix Read

Phoenix Read

© Copyright 2021 - All rights reserved.

The content contained within this book may not be reproduced, duplicated, or transmitted without direct written permission from the author or the publisher.

Under no circumstances will any blame or legal responsibility be held against the publisher, or author, for any damages, reparation, or monetary loss due to the information contained within this book, either directly or indirectly.

Legal Notice:

This book is copyright protected. It is only for personal use. You cannot amend, distribute, sell, use, quote, or paraphrase any part, or the content within this book, without the consent of the author or publisher.

Disclaimer Notice:

Please note the information contained within this document is for educational and entertainment purposes only. All effort has been executed to present accurate, up-to-date, reliable, complete information. No warranties of any kind are declared or implied. Readers acknowledge that the author is not engaged in the rendering of legal, financial, medical, or professional advice. The content within this book has been derived from various sources. Please consult a licensed professional before attempting any techniques outlined in this book.

By reading this document, the reader agrees that under no circumstances is the author responsible for any losses, direct or indirect, that are incurred due to the use of the information contained within this document, including, but not limited to, errors, omissions, or inaccuracies.

Table of Contents

Chapter 1: Introduction-Your Retirement Financial Planning Starts Here 6

What is the Best Approach for Couples? 8
When is the Best Time to Talk About Retirement Planning? 9
What Couples Need to Know 10
The Power of Compound Interest 12
The Phases of Retirement Financial Planning 22

Chapter 2: Couples' Goal - Communicating Your Dreams to Your Partner 25

Communicating Retirement Finances 26
Life Expectancy 28
Discuss and Understand Social Security 29
Factors That Affect Your Social Security Benefits 29
How to Increase Your Social Security Benefits 33
Insurance Through Retirement 35
Strategize to decrease your healthcare expenses 36
Guarding Against Financial Fraud 41
Where to Live After Retirement 45

Chapter 3: How to Avoid Common Pitfalls and Misconceptions 54

Common Delusions or Perceptions People Have About Retirement 54
Common Mistakes Couples Make with Their Retirement Planning 65

Chapter 4: Working on Your Visions for a Stress-Free Retirement 75

Challenges That Can Derail Your Stress-Free Retirement 76
Ease into Retirement 90
The Threat of Pension Contribution 91
Make the Most of Your Free Time 92
Beware of Dishonest Managers 93

Chapter 5: Managing Your Retirement Finances - Before and After Retirement 95

Sources of Retirement Income 96
The Dynamics of One Partner Working While the Other is Retired 120

Chapter 6: Leveraging on Various Retirement Rules for Seniors 125

Paying Down Debts in Retirement 125
Retirement Expenses for Couples 133
Impact of Interest Rates on Couples Financial Retirement Plans 139

Chapter 7: Understand Your Taxes and Grow Your Withdrawals During Retirement 143

Pros and Cons of Withdrawal from Your Retirement Accounts 143
The 4% Rule of Thumb for Retirement Withdrawals 149
Rules of Withdrawal Rate and Strategy 153
Estimating Taxes in Retirement 157

Chapter 8: Avoid the Risk of Drifting Apart After Retirement 162

Financial Reasons Why Couples Drift Apart 162
Estate Planning 167

Conclusion 177

A Plea From the Author 180

References 181

Chapter 1

Introduction-Your Retirement Financial Planning Starts Here

Retirement is the departure or withdrawal from an active working position due to age or physical disability. There is also a category of people who decide to retire when they're qualified for public or private pension benefits. However, others are forced to discontinue due to psychological conditions that no longer favors them to continue active service or due to some legalities.

Retirement is a recent development in most countries because it was introduced in the late 19th century. What we had before then was an arrangement where people continue to work until their death. This was also due to low life expectancy.

According to the Social Security Administration, The Germans were the first to introduce retirement age and benefits in 1889.

The term "retirement" brings relief and smiles to those who work 8-hours shifts. It usually denotes a time in their life when they would relax at home watching TV, reading newspapers on days that would have typically been a working day. For some others, retirement could mean spending more time with families and friends, traveling on a road trip, soaking up the sun, and peace all around.

Retirement is supposed to mark the end of a daily struggle for the salaried worker, especially if they have a retirement plan. It should even make life a lot easier for couples if they had planned their retirement together. Couples could live a financially independent life in their golden years with no concern for where the next salary would come from.

Hence, couples who desire financial independence and restful retirement years need to have solid retirement financial planning. This plan is not for one spouse to make but for all parties in the relationship. For couples in private corporations, their retirement plan would essentially be in their hands to control. A good retirement program would help you decide retirement income objectives and design a viable route to enjoy the advantages.

Retirement financial planning for couples is when spouses set retirement income goals, management plans/strategies and follow through with necessary actions to achieve these objectives.

What is the Best Approach for Couples ?

Couples often find it challenging to discuss their finances. This is one of the top reasons why couples break up.

The importance of communication cannot be overemphasized for couples planning the state of their finances for retirement. This communication must be deliberate.

The primary thing you must do as a couple is to share your financial retirement dreams, goals, and expectations. Couples frequently disagree about just how much money to save for retirement and if spouses should retire at the same time.

A recent study by the [2]Center for Retirement Research at Boston College revealed that couples with dual income are not saving more for retirement than other savers. In most households, only one partner has a retirement account. Dual-earning couples with only one saver might be saving less than they should for their retirement.

These are some of the issues that can impact your retirement financial planning as a family because they need to be addressed objectively. Communication will help couples align and have a clearer vision for their golden age.

The best approach for couples will be to talk deliberately about their retirement financial plans and the best strategy to apply.

When is the Best Time to Talk About Retirement Planning?

Often couples find it hard to agree on when to start their retirement financial planning. This can be due to how each party handles issues related to finances. A spouse or both might believe that talking about retirement is not a necessity at the moment, so they can go about their daily lives until they are older.

Another known challenge couples face with planning is, at what stage in their careers should they start taking their retirement issues seriously and deliberately plan for them?

Finally, age is a significant factor for couples when it comes to planning for retirement finances. Most couples like to wait till they are older or close to pulling out of active working life. Depending on your paycheck size, delaying your retirement financial planning to later years could mean a significant difference in the type of lifestyle you would be living when you are finally retired.

Retirement financial planning involves more than just incomes and assets; it also includes future expenses, liabilities, and life expectancy. So, like all plans, it needs to be done ahead of time. With an average work-life around 36 to 38 years, it's always best to start retirement plans as early as possible. When you have an early strategy, you can tweak it along the line, and you will be setting yourself up for a great retirement because you started early.

As couples in a long relationship, retirement finances should come up as early as possible into the relationship. Early planning is always better; however, it's never too late or early to start implementing your retirement plans.

What Couples Need to Know

Couples need to be informed about their retirement planning because it goes beyond just putting money aside for the golden age. How you treat your retirement financial planning is basically dependent on your knowledge, attitude, and information. Attitudes involve how partners take responsibilities and their financial risk tolerance. Suppose both partners tend to handle financial responsibilities for their future. In that case, they will be more likely to engage in retirement planning processes.

Younger couples tend to be more focused on the present rather than the future or starting early. Acquiring knowledge of retirement is not a significant concern to them, but that could be just what they need to make their latter years easier. For a holistic investment in retirement planning, young couples need to be financially literate. This is where the phrase "knowledge is power" comes to life.

Here's a list of what couples need to know for their retirement financial planning

- Age and length of service to retires for each spouse
- Present and future income taxes for each partner
- Available investment options
- Return on investment on and compound interest
- Risk and return of various investment
- Lifetime path of annual earnings and retirement income

The Power of Compound Interest

Compound interest is when the interest on your investment earns interest. The longer the time you have to invest, the more interest you will earn. If you start saving $150 per month, it would be worth three times more if you invest that at age 25 than if you had to wait till you are 45 years. This is the power of compound interest. Even if you can invest more cash in the future, you will never make up for the time lost and the interest you would have earned.

Common Questions Couples Encounter When Planning Retirement

Even after saving enough, couples should prepare for the fundamental change in lifestyles that may significantly affect their finances and relationships. Here are a few real questions that can guide you through these crucial financial and emotional discussions.

Should You Retire at the Same Time?

Couples should put it into consideration if it makes financial sense to retire at the same time. This decision is crucial because it has both emotional and economic implications. It may appear beautiful for both couples to retire at the same time. Still, financially, it makes more sense for one partner to work for a few more years.

One of the considerations here is that while one partner's earning reaches its peak, the other can work for some more years if no circumstances limit their ability. One partner working some years longer will have a significant difference on the couple's Social Security benefits eventually.

Another consideration is if they are both qualified for Medicare. Suppose one spouse is entitled to Medicare and the other is not. In that case, it may make financial sense for the younger partner to hang on to a job for healthcare benefits until they are eligible for Medicare.

This decision of one partner working a while longer than the other can create some challenges. However, excellent communication and strategy will help them figure out and agree that it works to the couple's advantage.

For some families, this question is a tricky one because you must factor in your financial preparedness and your physical abilities, how you or your spouse feels about their work. For example, for a spouse, retirement may mean a final escape from daily laboring; for the other, it may mean losing identity. It's not cast in stone that both of you must stop working at the same time. The timing is as crucial as it is for an individual as it is for the couple.

Where to Live After Retirement?

Retirement is not called "golden years" for nothing. It is the time for couples to enjoy doing what they love to do, like living their dreams. You can spend more time with family and serve the community amongst others. All these plans need to be in the couple's retirement financial plans.

You need to decide if living in your current city is cost-effective, or if you need to move to another. Knowing the best places to live after retirement early enough can go a long way. That way, you can start looking at mortgages and the best option for you and when to start. The significant factors that could influence your decision are:

- Home Prices
- Tax Rates
- Quality of the healthcare (especially for seniors)
- The overall cost of living in that city
- Move to the countryside or live in the city

You can find some of this information online, and maybe later, you can have an expert look into this to make an informed decision.

There's a lot to consider when attempting to answer this question; if you move to a less expensive city, it makes economic sense, but what about the proximity to family and friends? Will it be easy for the grandkids to come to visit? What is the emotional implication of moving to a retirement community?

The earlier couples take on these questions and answer them, the better their plans will begin to shape.

What do You do with Your Time?

A spouse often knows what they want to do when they are retired, but the story is not the same for couples. Couples should have their goals aligned.

Before retiring is the best time to plan what to do during retirement. Some factors will determine what each spouse can do.

Some ideas of what you could do include:

Learn Something New

Retirement years are a good time to learn something new. Couples can include affordable courses and studies they wish to take or even offer their knowledge to the community college. There are educational trips for seniors that can benefit the couples.

Start a Business

Couples can take advantage of their retirement years to start that business they have always wanted or convert that side hustle into a full-time business. How about offering their skills and experience as consultants?

Part-Time Job

As part of their retirement financial planning, couples need to decide if they would take on a part-time job. This job will not only add extra income to the family, but it gives them a place to socialize now and then. They can find a part-time job that offers insurance and other benefits.

Volunteer

Couples can include in their plans to use their retirement age to give back to society. There are organizations like churches and NGOs, local and international, always in need of skilled volunteers.

Alternatively, you could decide to represent your community in the political process or serve on a school board.

Write A Book

There is no better time for couples to write a book than during retirement. Couples can write books about just anything, from sharing their life stories and experience to about any other topics. This could also be another source of income in the long run.

To avoid conflicts that lead to breakups during retirement, both of you must discuss and work together on this path.

Keep Fit

Couples should get involved in activities that will help their body stay fit. Physical exercises are good but not to the extreme level. Other activities that will help a great deal include golfing, yoga, jogging, walking, etc.

How Important is Your Time "Together?"

Time is all that you both have when retired; well, that's the assumption. The common challenge for retiree couples is how much time they want to spend together or alone. A partner may want to spend more time volunteering, taking classes, or being involved in sport. In contrast, the other wants to just be around the other person.

Talk about how much personal space and respect for each other's time needs to be during retirement. If you respect each other's alone time, you will value your time together.

How do you Manage Household Finances?

For couples who have been together for a long time, it's likely you already have a hang of everyday expenses. However, many couples are yet to figure out how to manage their finances, which needs to be sorted, so it doesn't become a big problem during retirement. What will it be? is it a "yours, mine, and ours" approach? With this method, each person has a certain amount dedicated to them and another for the family.

This stage is where you need to revisit your budgets and income sources because you will be going from saving to spending. Ensure you have enough to cover the essentials. In your financial retirement plans, endeavor to make at least two years of "living expenses" available in an accessible account.

How Much Debt Should You Carry into Retirement?

It would be best to be debt-free by the time you are retiring; however, this is not the case for most couples. It's a desirable dream but hardly realistic. So, do all you can to settle all high-interest debts like car loans and credit cards; and from now on, agree only to buy what you can pay off within a month.

For Mortgages, the situation is different. Interest on a mortgage may drop low, and tax-deductible and this could work in your favor. However, if being free of a mortgage burden will give you peace during retirement, paying off your mortgage would be the best option.

The lesser the debts you carry into retirement, the more likely you will live your dream lifestyle.

When is the Best Time to Take Social Security?

Though this is a personal choice, couples should carefully consider how it may influence their general benefits; short-term, long-term, and survivors. Broadly, the longer you wait (up to age 70) to claim benefits, the higher your payout. However, you will find a few approaches that could raise your benefits based upon your income and age.

For example, a low earner may take advantage early, while the higher earner waits until age 70. The spousal benefits can also be a variable for nonworking or even lower-earning spouses. To have a basic idea of your choices, run a few figures on a Social Security calculator and then speak with your financial advisor.

How Often is Best to Revisit Your Investment Portfolio

As you plan your retirement finances, you will know more about investment portfolios and how to manage them. It's ok to take on more risk when you are both still far from retiring, but it's wiser to start reducing your investment risk as you begin to settle into retirement.

There's a method to it. Here's a suggested timeline that works pretty well;

- Pre-retirement - Strive for a moderate approach of 60% stock, 35% fixed income, and 5% Cash.
- Early Retirement - You might want to shift the figures around a bit - 40% stock, 50% fixed income, and 10% cash
- Late Retirement - 20% Stock, 50% fixed income and 30% cash

Retirement in most cases lasts several decades; hence it's crucial to consider investing in stocks to help mitigate against inflation. How much you wish to invest not only depends on your wealth but also your risk appetite. Both couples need to agree on this because individuals always have different approaches to investments and risks.

What to do About Health Issues

Health issues are unfortunate, unforeseen circumstances that can potentially dig a hole in a couple's finances. Ensure to continue to fund your Health Saving Account for future use because once you file for Social Security, you will no longer be allowed to fund your HSA. On retirement, ensure you have a great Medigap or Medicare Advantage Policy.

Consider long-term care insurance in your planning phase. Lastly, agree on essential estate planning and be sure to have advanced healthcare directives.

Who Gets What When You are Gone?

This subject can be a bit sensitive for couples to talk about, but it's too crucial to be looked over. Couples need to talk about their beneficiaries. It is essential to name who will get what from retirement accounts, banks, insurance, and other income sources. To ensure their wishes are carried out to the latter, there must be a Will that supports their wishes.

It gets a bit complicated if one or both spouses have been involved financially with exes from previous relationships. Also, in divorces and other types of relationships, couples can agree on what goes to who. For instance, a spouse may not want their IRA savings to go to their partner if they are divorced, but the case may differ if children are involved.

These are some of the crucial conversations couples need to have when planning their finances for retirement.

The Phases of Retirement Financial Planning

As couples, when you discuss your retirement financial plans, you need to know that a proper plan is divided into three phases; investment, accumulation, and withdrawal phases.

Accumulation Phase

This is the time you are actively investing and saving towards your retirement. It's the foundation of everything because it will largely determine the type of lifestyle you will live during your retirement years.

Couples in long-term relationships need to be very deliberate about this phase and plan together, monitor their investment and saving, and ensure it's growing steadily.

Planning, Preparation, and Preservation Phase

Here is the heart of your retirement planning efforts, ideally addressed about a decade before your retirement date. This phase will have a summary of; your entire retirement investments, expected essential living expenditures, lifestyle expenditures, possible tax duties, Social Security benefits commencement date, any anticipated retirement, Required Minimum Distribution calculations for fund qualified for, retirement risk-profile, health and medical planning needs, and future debt reduction before actually retiring.

You should pay close attention to your anticipated retirement cost of living and consider your essential monthly expenses, your preferred lifestyle, and how the cost of inflation might change your future earnings.

Distribution Phase

Also known as the withdrawal phase, it's the purpose of all your planning; to benefit from income streams you have created to last longer than your lifetime. This phase starts when you stop earning regular paid income. This is when your phase one and phase two efforts begin to pay off; you begin to get Social Security benefits, planned income from your investments, and potential pension.

What you have saved up for this phase will determine the type of lifestyle you will live for the rest of your life.

Chapter 2

Couples' Goal - Communicating Your Dreams to Your Partner

Having a different retirement goal and objective from your spouse is not uncommon. However, planning together and aligning your goals should be more exciting. The dream of giving up an active work life and focusing on the things you enjoy doing is one every adult looks forward to, even more so for couples.

Creating a balance in your goals, reaching a compromise, and having a unified front as you plan towards retirement can lead to a fulfilling retirement. Much has been said about how couples find it hard to agree. Imagine if you and your partner work on breaking this hurdle and start early. Starting early and discussing your financial plans will give you a great advantage.

Understanding what each person would love will go a long way in achieving shared aspirations and where you need to strike a balance.

Communicating Retirement Finances

Couples often talk about household incomes and expenditures, but the same zeal is lacking when it comes to retirement.

The statistics are a bit disturbing. According to a [3]Prudential study published in Financial Reporter;

- 24% of couples agreed they have never discussed retirement income plans with their spouses
- 67% of couples have no idea what their combined retirement income will look like, and a fifth have never even disclosed their exact income to their partner
- Nearly 46% of couples fear they would run out of cash during retirement.
- 20% are concerned about their inability to support their children or grandchildren when they retire.
- 15% are also worried about paying too much tax in retirement. On the other hand, a whopping 28% of couples do not concern themselves with retirement financial planning matters as couples.

- Despite most couples having concerns about retirement financial planning, almost 73% of couples have not taken advantage of the pension rules.
- Disturbingly, 9% of women agreed they would rely solely on their partner's or parents' income, compared to only 2% of men. Another 10% of couples say they have no retirement savings and rely on the government for their income.

Stan Russell, a retirement expert at Prudential, breaks it down succinctly;

"Conversations about finances are never easy, especially if you have not even told your partner how much you earn. It is extremely important to discuss your finances, however, as it is essential to know where you both stand so you can plan for a comfortable retirement.

"Couples who don't talk, and make joint plans, risk losing out on making the most of the pension saving tax relief available between them, not using their full allowances in retirement may also end up with unrealistic expectations of what their savings combined are worth.

"For couples who have never had conversations regarding their personal finances, it is best to seek advice from a professional financial adviser who should be able to inform

them of the best way they can maximize their savings and use new pension rules if appropriate."

The starting point is to understand what income and assets you need to fund your retirement. These include; fixed income, savings, investments, property, defined contribution pension, final salary pensions, and state pension. Both partners need to understand the other's approach to retirement financing.

Life Expectancy

One crucial aspect during the communication process is talking about life expectancy; your optimal retirement age depends on your life expectancy. Terminal illnesses like cancer, stroke, and heart diseases have influenced life expectancies in the U.S. For babies born in 2014, life expectancy is almost 70 years, so if you hit 65, your life expectancy can increase.

Understanding your life expectancy can help you plan enough resources to take care of yourself after retirement; otherwise, your income sources may grow lean over time.

Discuss and Understand Social Security

Social Security benefits are a vital component of your retirement plan. Couples need to understand how it works and how to take advantage of the opportunities.

Quick suggestions:

- If it's possible, work at least 35 years.
- Barring any health restrictions, work until you reach your full retirement age.

To be eligible for 100% payment of your Social Security benefits, you will need to work until you reach your Full Retirement Age (FRA). This suggests that while you may be eligible to start receiving social security benefits at 62, it would be wise if you can work a while longer so your monthly income can keep growing.

For partners who intend on taking their full retirement benefits, it's essential to be aware of your full retirement age.

Factors That Affect Your Social Security Benefits

Besides working your full retirement age, there are number of factors that affect what you receive as Social Security benefits:

Number of Active Years and Contribution to Social Security

For all your active working years, your earnings are recorded in the Social Security System. You will get full benefits if there are no gaps in your employment history. Gaps can occur due to illnesses, working and not paying Social security, unemployment, or caregiving.

Earning During Active Contribution to Social Security

To qualify for benefits, you need to contribute to Social Security and earn 40 credits for ten working years. Your monthly benefit is on your lifetime earnings. Your 35 years' highest documented earning years are also considered. Boosting your earnings with contributions from other earnings may enhance your benefits because there's a correlation between higher earning and higher monthly benefits.

When You Want To Start Receiving Your Benefits

If you choose monthly benefits before your full retirement age, your benefit will be lower, and you will continue to receive lower benefits over your lifetime. However, if you take your benefits after your full retirement age, you are set for a larger monthly payment. It gets even better if you decide to take your benefits at age 70 instead of 62; you are guaranteed a 75% return on your benefits. There are very few investments out there that can match such returns.

Peculiar Situations to Consider

Knowing when to take your Social Security benefits is crucial. Your time will be dependent on your values, vision of your retirement life, and your specific lifestyle as a couple. Think about these life scenarios and their effect:

Active Working Years

If you take benefits early while you continue to work, your benefits may be reduced. Alternatively, if you work until your full retirement age, you may receive your full benefits.

Your Tax Liability

According to the Social Security Administration, about 40% of people who claim monthly benefits have to pay taxes on them. Up to 85% of your benefits may be taxable, depending on the tax bracket you fall into.

Health Challenges

If you and your spouse have a history of good health, your retirement benefits may last longer than you imagined. Hence, it's essential to know your life expectancy to decide when to claim your benefits and get the maximum amount. Conversely, If you or your spouse suffer poor health, it may result in an early Social Security claim.

Marital Status

Your marital status: married or divorced has implications on your benefits.

- A spouse can receive half of her divorced partner's full benefits if married for ten years or more and not remarried. With this, you can claim your spouse's benefits earlier and postpone yours till a later date.
- For couples still married, the spouse with lower earnings can claim benefits earlier while delaying the higher earner's benefits until they reach full retirement age or later.

How to Increase Your Social Security Benefits

Here are a few steps you can take to enjoy the maximum amount possible on your social security benefits:

- Your Social Security benefits are calculated on the 35 years where you have worked and earned income. If there are gaps in the 35 years, your payout will be reduced.

- Work until you reach the full retirement age of 66 or 67 to get a total payout. The monthly payment for people who retire before the full retirement age is significantly reduced.

- Increase your income by adding another job or getting a raise; this will boost the amount you will receive from Social Security when you retire.

- You can sometimes delay claiming your Social Security benefits until you get to 70. There's an annual 8% increase for every year you delay until you get to 70.

- Suppose you have dependents under the age of 19. In that case, you can claim up to one-half additional Social Security payments on your full retirement benefits.

- Spouses can claim benefits based on their work record or up to 50% of the higher earner's benefit, whichever is higher. If you were married for at least ten years, you could also claim Social Security benefits based on an ex-spouse's work record.

- Manage your Social Security Taxes. If the total of your gross income, half of your Social Security benefits, and non-taxable interest, are higher than $25,000 for a partner and $32,000 for couples, up to 50% of your Social Security benefits could be taxable. Suppose an individual's income is more than $34,000, or couples $44,000. In that case, income tax could be calculated on as much as 85% of your Social Security benefits.

- Retirees can boost the amount the surviving spouse will receive by delaying claiming Social Security. When one member of a married couple dies, the surviving spouse can inherit the deceased spouse's benefit payment if it's more than his or her current benefit.

- Monitor your Social Security account and ensure your work history is adequately updated. Make your work count.

Insurance Through Retirement

Know your values, the quality of lifestyle, and dependence on other people for making healthcare choices.

Stay active (or have your partner work) before full retirement age or even more to keep up your wellbeing care coverage through a company.

Save out-of-pocket expenses and also have a strategy concerning which income resources will be utilized to cover healthcare.

Strategize to decrease your healthcare expenses

Your medical care expenses during retirement will turn out to be among the bigger groups in your budget. Their influence on the way you live could be significant due to healthcare costs increasing over the cost of living adjustments that many retirees receive.

For all these reasons, it helps to know what costs you could incur during your retirement, the choices available to help cover your expenses, and strategies to lower your costs.

[4]Fidelity Investments' study estimates health care during retirement to cost $260,000 for a 65-year-old couple in 2016. This figure doesn't include the cost of long-term care.

Unlike what's obtainable during your active years, where your employer's health care plan primarily covers you, your health needs will become your sole responsibility and a large portion of your spending during retirement.

Cut Down Your Debt Burden

This is a crucial aspect of retirement financial planning that couples need to review and make adjustments. Before you retire, ensure both parties get the hang of their spending and borrowing habits because that's a significant way to avoid spontaneous and indiscriminate borrowing that affects your retirement finances.

Here are some general recommendations to help your stay focused on your financial planning towards debt reduction;

- Spend less than 30% of your credit limits
- Avoid delinquency and pay your bills on time. Where you can't pay off everything, pay down high-interest debt balances.
- Have an emergency fund made up of at least three months of living expenses.
- Document all your spending and look for where you can block "leaks" and save more.
- Don't spend more than you earn. This helps you save before and during retirement.

A study by the PEW titled [5] "The Complex Story of American Debt" revealed that roughly 80% of Americans have some debt type. Therefore, if you're nearing retirement or are retired and in debt, then you are probably not alone. Your challenge will be to deal with that debt tactfully.

As you begin to work deliberately on your financial retirement plan, be deliberate about debt reduction. Spouses can even check one other to ensure the other is not piling up debts. At the same time, another is committed to reducing it. Use the next ten years to your retirement to pay off your debts and redirect your spending habit to debt reduction.

- A mortgage is likely the biggest monthly expense you have on your list. Pay it off before retirement if you can. Make extra payments monthly towards reducing the principal balance and interest so you can gain more equity.

- If you have other high-interest debt burdens, pay them first before your mortgage.

- Direct more payment towards reducing your debts than retirement contributions. If your debt costs more than your investment, it only makes sense to direct more funds to pay off the debts.

- Resist the urge and temptation of taking new loans. Loan offers are always available and presented in a very attractive manner. Often spouses accept these offers before they inform their partners. For a debt-free retirement period, you need to resist these offers. Think long-term and pay for what you buy instantly.

- Suppose you have debts that follow you into retirement by chance. In that case, you may consider taking a part-time job or working full retirement age so you can have more income to cover your debt obligations.

- When you must use credit, ensure you read the terms and conditions about fees and timing.

- You can use your home equity loan to reduce your debt load.

- Refinance your mortgage or move to a rental apartment

Co-signing Loans for Family and Friends

Family and friends with poor credit scores always search for co-signers when they want to take a loan. This is another critical aspect of your retirement planning you need to discuss with your spouse. For retirement financial planning, always apply caution before taking on debts that require you to co-sign for other people.

- When you co-sign any loan, it means you are taking legal responsibility for the debt if the other person defaults.

- When the primary borrower misses or delays payment, it will harm your credit and possibly prevent you from borrowing in the future.

- When you co-sign a loan, you are fully responsible for the total debt, all interest accrued, and the legal fees incurred during recovery.

- Co-signing can affect your Social Security benefits. It can be used to repay your loan, which would consequently interrupt your retirement income.

- You cannot get out of a co-signed debt until it is fully paid off.

The decision to co-sign could be tricky, especially if based on relationships, emotions, and favors. However, know that it's your credit at risk, and it may ultimately affect your income.

Guarding Against Financial Fraud

Prevention against fraud is an aspect of retirement financial planning that couples ignore a lot. It later comes to bite them. This has to be a critical aspect of your planning, so you don't end up planning so well, paying off debt, building streams of income, then losing them to fraudsters.

Seniors whom friends, families, and fraudsters exploited in recent years have lost an average of $34,200. This is according to a report by the U.S. [6]Consumer Financial Protection Report.

According to this report, Seniors suffer losses in different forms; It can come in the form of a child stealing their parent's money because they have a power of attorney or are in charge of their parents' benefits. In some cases, it's the caregiver who is writing herself a more extensive check in the name of getting paid. Other cases involve love fraud, where a lover is requesting a huge sum from a senior to help facilitate her travels to visit him.

In 2017 there were 63,500 reports of fraudulent activities that year alone, four times as many as in 2013. Losses suffered by the elderly totaled $1.7 billion.

The statistics get even scarier.

- Outside analysts looking at elder fraud have separately estimated losses in the range of $2.9 billion to $36.5 billion a year.

- Seniors ages 80 and older suffered the second-highest average loss, $39,200.

- Seniors ages 60-69 had the third-highest, $22,700.

- Seniors ages 50-59 had the lowest, $13,400.

- In 51% of cases, strangers were identified as responsible for fraudulent activities.

- About 14% of the reports didn't specify who was responsible for the suspected fraud.

- In 36% of cases, the victims knew the bad actors, be they a fiduciary or a family member.

A fiduciary has the legal responsibility to manage another person's assets or benefits. They can be a trustee, guardian, or someone with power of attorney.

The report further states that the retired losses are mostly significant where a fiduciary is involved; it's up to $83,600 per victim. Where a non-family member like a caregiver was the culprit, the loss is around $57,800; If it was a family member who is cheating their elderly out of their money, the average was $42,700. For a total stranger, the loss was $17,000.

Guidelines for Avoiding and Detecting fraud

Retirement preparation encompasses many areas of handling your life. An important area to research is the way you safeguard yourself and your money from fraud. This is particularly critical once you think about financial fraud's income-reducing conditions when new income sources are somewhat restricted.

- The older couples get, the more likely they are to be targeted by fraudsters. Be careful who you trust with your finances.

- Don't be in a hurry to sign off on a financial decision. Take your time, discuss with your partner and trusted people or professionals before you conclude a deal.

- Beware of pressure tactics that offer "too-good-to-be-true" deals. Remember the saying, "if it is too good to be true, then it probably is."

- Contact legal authorities if you suspect any irregular activities on your financial records.

- Destroy all documents with sensitive information if they are no longer needed

- Review your billing statements and accounts regularly for unauthorized and strange charges.

- Make it a habit to review your credit reports to understand the activities going on there.

- Keep an eye on the financial institution's alerts and ensure the information you got corresponds with what you authorized.

- Guard your financial and personal details carefully, for example, your social security number, date of birth, credit and debit card numbers, and others.

- For your digital activities, use strong passwords and change them often. Avoid sharing your password with anyone.

- Install apps that reveal caller IDs so you can identify any caller before you answer their calls.
- Don't stay too long on the phone with strangers. They may be phishing for information that will harm you.

You can proactively put these measures in place before you retire; this way, it would have been a habit to help safeguard you from losing your hard-earned income.

Where to Live After Retirement

One of the most significant decisions in working couples' lives is agreeing on when they retire from the active workforce. The next big decision would be where to make your new home.

Retirement gives you the freedom to choose where you wish to live instead of being tied to a particular location for proximity to the workplace. However, before you pack and head out to your new place, couples need to consider the implication of such a decision on their families, lifestyle, commitments, healthcare, and others.

There are some factors to consider before making the final decision on your next destination.

Your Cost of Living

When working with limited funds in investment accounts and Social Security to last you the rest of your lifetime, you cannot afford to overspend on home or other essential expenditures.

Regrettably, in some countries, your basic needs will cost a lot more. Living in the costliest cities will require an income higher than $10,000 greater than the cheapest ones to pay for the essentials.

Suppose you reside in a state with a higher cost of living, like Massachusetts, Hawaii, Maryland, or New York, Paris, Tokyo, London, Geneva. In that case, you might want to consider moving somewhere where your money can stretch much farther.

Where to live is a significant expense on your budget. The average pre-retiree is expected to spend 55% to 80% of their current income in retirement. Getting a low cost of living and affordable home is crucial to couples so their savings can be stretched further.

Not every location is cost-friendly to retirees. According to a study by Blacktower Financial Management, Mississippi, Oklahoma, Arkansas, Missouri, and Tennessee, are some states with the lowest cost of living in the U.S. Hawaii, California, New York, Massachusetts, and Oregon, are the most expensive.

For housing consideration, West Virginia, Mississippi, Arkansas, Oklahoma, and Indiana offer the lowest average property prices. While Hawaii, California, Massachusetts, and New

York has the highest property prices.

According to International Living in its [7]2021 Annual Global Retirement Index. The best 10 places to retire are Vietnam, Malta, France, Malaysia, Ecuador, Portugal, Columbia, Mexico, Panama, and Costa Rica.

Travel Before You Choose

In checking for the best locations to live or move to, a few places will appeal to you. Take time out to visit these locations and spend a few days to see things for yourself. Both partners should ask the right questions and don't assume anything.

Most locals are friendly to visitors, so take time to visit the neighborhood and talk to real people. Ask them as many questions as you desire, check out recreational activities, nightlife, healthcare, and how they treat seniors. Talk to realtors physically, visit some home options and see for yourself. You might even find a passionate person willing to help you find a good place when you finally decide.

Research and Ask Questions Before You Move

The decision of where to move to is so vital that you need to do a little more work than usual so you can arrive at a choice that suits the family;

- Start from the internet. Check the economic development, crime rates, and recent development in the state via the internet. Visit the local chamber of commerce and the website dedicated to visitors. All these should give you ideas of the population, weather, local attractions, and quality of life. When you have the time, take a trip with your partner, and spend a few days seeing things yourself.

- Check out the cost of living. Information about the cost of living in most cities of the world is available online. Check and look out for real-life stories of people living in these locations. Some websites even have calculators you can use to compare.

- Check out the crime rate. You can easily find reports on local crime rates online. Additionally, the [8]FBI's Uniform Crime Reporting Program provides information on the crime rates in all big and small cities in the U.S. For other cities around the world, the Interpol website will be a great source of information.

- Healthcare facilities for seniors. Checkout of the city has good healthcare facilities for seniors. How close are they, and what type of specialty do they handle?

Consider Staying Where You Are

In some cases, opting and leaving for another location could be a lot costlier than staying where you have always lived while working. Think about it, compare all the conditions, and staying where you are might be a better solution. If your current home is affordable, has the right amenities you need, is close to family and friends, and you are mortgage-free, then there will be no need to opt and leave for the sake of it.

Alternatively, you can make a local move by selling your current home at a profit, cut down on your bills and maintenance costs. You could then buy something a little less expensive. That way, you can have some cash.

If you have the means, you can try a new location with a condo in the city and a house in the country. Buying a second home before retirement can help you test your options. You can rent the house in the high season and visit in the off-season. This would have helped you get extra cash while you decide if it's a place you want to live in after retirement.

Familiarize With Your Taxes

A major component in the financial planning for couples when deciding where to live is taxation. There are some considerations to look in;

State Taxes: some states do not have personal state income taxes, while others have.

Taxes on Retirement Income: The states of Hawaii, Illinois, Mississippi, and Pennsylvania exempt most or all retirement income such as Social Security benefits from taxation. In some other states, retirement and pension incomes are taxed. While a few others provide tax credits for these types of retirement incomes. Check and be familiar with what is obtainable in your desired state.

Choosing a state with a lower tax rate does not mean the cost of living there is also lower. However, if you find a state with lower taxes, lower cost of living, and lower property tax, then that's a real deal that will save you money.

Consider life planning over tax planning. If you are unhappy about where you live and how you are spending your retirement, low taxes will not make you happy. Lower taxes do not necessarily mean saving much money.

Think About Amenities for Retirees

Often, we see couples want to move away from civilization to a secluded area to reduce their expenses, but after a short while, one person starts to feel isolated, detached from their everyday life.

Couples should plan to retire to a place with high livability indicators like a vibrant economy, where you can get a job to support your finances or help you stay socialized, a place with mild weather, low crime, and has access to the internet to keep you informed.

Top among the amenities you want to look out for would include hospitals and adult daycare, assisted living facilities, and wellness opportunities. Areas with easy access to golf courses, fitness centers, ski resorts, and the likes will be a nice place to settle in for.

The top places to retire also have attributes that attract newcomers, like retail and art places, public libraries, and civic associations. Natural endowments, for example, recreational property and historical landmarks, can make your stay more memorable.

Given their cultural, recreational, and educational resources, in addition to accessibility to elite university associations, college towns are becoming more and more popular retirement destinations. Universities attract newcomers by default. The cities surrounding them always have greater public transit systems and better rental markets than other towns. Many major cities also often match these criteria and are inclined to be relatively recession-proof and retiree-friendly.

Walkable Areas

Transportation may be a massive cost for seniors. Locating an area where you can walk to most areas makes it possible to cut down this price. In reality, if you discover an extremely walkable place, you might even have the ability to eliminate a car or truck. This can save you thousands of dollars annually in registration, gas, and maintenance expenditures, and it frees you from squandering hard-earned retirement money on a car loan. It can also serve as a form of physical exercise which is good for the body.

Choosing a nearby place is also a fantastic idea since you might lose your ability to drive as you gradually enter deep into the years of your retirement. Suppose you are not at a nearby location. In that case, this may indicate the end of your liberty and the requirement to move to assisted living. However, if you're able to walk to places easily, you could have the ability to remain in your house a little longer.

Chapter 3

How to Avoid Common Pitfalls and Misconceptions

Common Delusions or Perceptions People Have About Retirement

Couples Think They Will Retire Debt-Free, but the Reality is Different

According to a survey by [9]Bankers Life Center for a Secure Retirement, 8 in 10 middle-income Baby Boomers have an annual income between $25,000 and $100,000, and less than $1,000,000 in investable assets now have some form of debt. A study from Pew Research Center supported that survey, showing that 80% of boomers had debt, and the median amount was more than $70,000. See the breakdown below;

- Millennials: 86% with a median debt of $46,000
- Generation X: 89% with a median debt of $103,800
- Baby Boomers: 80% with a median debt of $70,102
- Silent Generation: 58% with a median debt of $30,000

Additionally, According to data released from the Federal Reserve Bank of New York, Many boomers have more debt than ever. The average 65-year old borrower now holds 47% more in mortgage debt and 29% auto debt than a 65-year old did in 2003.

Yet, the Bankers Life data revealed that more than 53% of non-retired, middle-income boomers think they will retire without debt. Many average boomers embrace this common delusion: that they will retire without a debt burden.

However, what is obtainable in reality is different. Middle-income boomers have too much debt to be able to pay them off before they finally retire. According to the data, more than 28% (1 in 4) of boomers now devote over 40% of their monthly income to debt settlement, and about 23% have a mortgage with more than 20 years left.

The expert believes debt payment should take up more than 10% of your income.

The data further revealed that it's unlikely boomers will pay off their debt before they enter retirement. Less than one in four retired individuals say they are debt-free.

Boomers are likely to retire with a pile of debts. Below is the percentage of ages 52 to 75 who have one kind of debt;

- Credit Card Debts: Nearly 60% of non-retired and 48% of retired
- Mortgage: 48% non-retired and almost 40% retired
- Auto Loan: 32% retired and 34% non-retired
- Student and personal loans are other types of loans carried into retirement.

Only 23% retired and 18% non-retired have no form of debt.

Having some form of debt in retirement is not mainly a bad thing to worry about; just have a plan to pay off. Many retirees get to pay off their debts as they settle into retirement.

The challenge is that debt is likely to throw a wedge into the wheel of your dream retirement lifestyle. Debt is a financial obligation that should not be avoided or pushed aside till another time. Debt limits the type of financial freedom you have planned for your family. Couples will spend more dollars paying off debt during retirement than they planned.

Perceptions of Retirement Preparedness Vary

A study from the Federal Reserve finds individuals of different ages have a savings threshold that gives them a feeling that they are on track to get a decent retirement. For all those in retirement, reported economic well-being varies considerably with the motive for retirement.

According to the Federal Reserve, many adults approaching retirement are worried that they are not on track with their retirement financial planning. Retirement strategies differ by age, couples, and individuals. In its Survey of [10]Household Economics and Decision Making (SHED), the study revealed that 36% of non-retired persons think their retirement planning is on track, 44% say it is not on track, while the rest are unsure. It gets even interesting;

- One-quarter of the non-retired indicate that they have no financial retirement plans.

- Of the non-retired age 60 plus, 13% have no retirement savings or pension.

- For those non-retirees with no retirement savings or contributions like 401K or 403B was very common.

- 54% of non-retirees have money in this type of savings

- Only 22% of non-retiree say they have a defined benefit pension plan

Older couples are more likely to have retirement savings and stay on track than younger couples. Still, among those in active service in their 60s, 13% do not have any retirement savings or financial planning; about 45% think they are on track with their savings for retirement.

How couples self-assess their readiness depends on the amount they have saved and how long before they retire. Adults older than 30 naturally believe they are on track if they have $10,000 in savings for retirement. Meanwhile, the amount required in savings increases with age. Adults 45 to 59 who believe their retirement financial planning is on track typically have $250,000 saved away. Those between 30 and 44 think they're on track with $100,000 savings.

Only about two in ten non-retirees younger than 45 have retirement savings that meet their age limit. The fraction rises with age to 27% of adults ages 45 to 59. The threshold for most to view savings as on track increases more rapidly with age than the fraction reaching that level of retirement savings.

Generally, more than 5% of non-retirees had to borrow from their retirement account before they retired. 4% withdrew the funds permanently, while 1% have done both. Those who withdrew before retirement are unlikely to see their plans as "on track" than those who have not.

Managing Financial Retirement and Financial Literacy

The level of comfort and knowledge in managing financial retirement plans differed among non-retirees and retired. Six out of ten non-retirees with financial retirement plans displayed a low comfort level in handling investment decisions.

Your self-assessed comfort in financial decisions may or may not tally with your actual knowledge. To understand individuals' financial awareness, respondents to the SHED survey were asked five standard questions to measure financial literacy; the average number of correct responses was 2.8, and 22% of adults got all five questions correct.

Using the measures above, those who demonstrated confidence in managing their retirement plans also expressed more financial knowledge. People with self-directed retirement accounts express comfort in decision-making in their response to the questions (3.7 out of 5) than those who express little or no comfort (2.9 out of 5).

Financial Well-Being in Retirement

One-quarter of adults see themselves as being retired. The report further reveals that retirees include every person who considers themselves retired despite having done some paid jobs in specific capacities. 17% of retirees say they have done some work for pay or profit before.

Retirees are more inclined to report they are doing fine financially (78%) than non-retirees (74%). Retirees that are working record even higher degrees of well-being. Almost half of the people in 2018 retired before age 62, also one-fourth retired between 62 and 64.

In general, early retirees report comparable levels of financial well-being as later retirees.

In determining when to retire, a desire to do other things than active work, or to spend some time with family, would be the most frequent factors. But, four in 10 retirees before age 62 and three in 10 between ages 62 and 64 stated that bad health contributed to their retirement. Over one-fifth of individuals who retired before age 65 say the absence of accessible work contributed to their choice.

The analysis found financial well-being varies substantially by the factors for retirement. In ten couples, nine stated doing something was quite crucial in their retirement choice to do fine financially, versus over half of individuals who retired because of bad health.

Retirement: The Realities Vs. Delusion

Fact: 59% of non-retirees planned to leave active service gradually, yet only 22% of retirees followed through.

Retirement itself is shrouded by a host of hearsay, fears, delusions, and false assumptions. When you hear the topic of retirement, what does it mean to you? Take note of the things that come to mind, write them down, and imagine yourself at retirement age.

If you are younger than 40, your responses will be different from people older than you. Your answer might well include terms like "future," "old age," there are signs that show that this topic is not relevant to you at this stage of your life.

If you fall in the older age bracket, the chances are you would have had some passing thought about retirement, and you would have associated with some of these concepts;

- Losing my earning power

- Losing my identity
- Enjoying financial independence
- Doing what I have always wanted to do
- I do not ever plan to retire
- Freedom from the daily grind
- Being useless
- Dependency and declining health

Whichever opinion you have about the above, they do not tell the whole story about retirement. Several expectations we have about retirement do not match the real thing.

According to the 2013 [11]Risks and Process of Retirement Survey by the Society of Actuaries;

- Of the pre-retirees surveyed, 38% expected to work until at least 65. Another 15% expected not to retire at all. Yet 54% of the retirees surveyed had retired before age 60.
- Many pre-retirees, 59%—planned to stop working gradually. Yet only 22% of retirees had done so. While 35% of pre-retirees intended to keep working part-time, only 10% of retirees did.

Little wonder many workers plan to stay actively employed; they need the money. Research in 2015 by the [12]Transamerica Retirement Survey of Workers estimates the median amount working adults in their 50s saved for retirement at merely $117,000. For workers 60 years and above, it is $172,000. Even when you add that to the Social Security benefits, that is hardly enough to support an adequate retirement lifestyle.

Even if you work and earn until you are 80 years old, your plans may still be unachievable. When organizations downsize, the older workers are the first target to be laid off. Health challenges for you, your partner, or your family member may also force you to retire unexpectedly. We cannot give up on retirement financial planning because our plans can be derailed. There are few ideas we can follow in dealing with the realities of retirement.

- Couples need to save as much as they can. Make funding retirement your priority, especially if it is too late to start early. Cut your spending, downsize, and pay off debt. Having more money in retirement gives you more options when bad things do happen.

- Improve your health: lose weight, exercise more, and eat a healthy diet. Improve your odds for staying well by changing what is within your power to change.

- Look at the whole retirement picture. Become willing to consider both the negative and positive possibilities to plan appropriately. Unreasonable pessimism and fear are no more realistic than unreasonable optimism.

In conclusion, the most acceptable approach may be accepting that retirement is no more or less predictable than any other phase of life. It's almost impossible to predict how healthy you or your spouse will be at 70 or if either of you will live till 100. While it is essential to have solid retirement financial planning, it is equally vital to enjoying the present.

Common Mistakes Couples Make with Their Retirement Planning

Couples work as a team to plan other aspects of their lives like chores, social calendars, etc. However, that power of unison is not exhibited to achieve the most critical milestones in their lives. When it comes to planning for their golden years, the number of couples who fail to communicate and successfully strategize is dwindling.

This is an unfortunate truth. We have more couples who talk about everything, but when it comes to finances, it becomes a no-go area; it turns out to be delicate and toxic.

Retirement planning can be challenging for some, but there are solutions to all the challenges you would face in the process. Below are some of the common mistakes couples make with their retirement planning;

Couples Don't Save Enough for Retirement

As previously mentioned, one in three couples in a relationship reported that neither they nor their spouse had started saving for retirement. This is a significant challenge across the board. We have primarily a situation where partners have individual plans and run blindly without carrying the other along, or where one partner believes the spouse's plan will be sufficient for both of them during retirement.

Couples do not just need to start saving, but they need to start saving early together. Retirement planning has to be built into the family system as early as possible. Where couples have different incomes, they need to work together to determine how they will support their financial retirement goals.

The best way will be to work with a retirement expert who can help you with a professional plan and execute it effectively.

Couples Don't Talk About How to Achieve their Retirement Dreams

More couples have shared their retirement dreams, like when they would love to retire, what they want to do during retirement, their desired lifestyle, and where they would love to live.

However, the specifics and how to achieve those lofty dreams are lacking. There are no plans in place to ensure those big pictures or goals happen. The failure to get into these plans is usually blamed on procrastination. Still, the challenge with retirement is that the longer you put away the plans for another day, the bigger and tougher the challenge becomes.

There are significant advantages like compounding interest and investment returns you can enjoy if you start early. Start by setting a proper budget for your retirement and start that today.

Couples Don't Carry Each Other Along

It is alarming that most couples leave each other in the dark on financial issues. Each person wants to exercise complete control over their money. For instance, many couples have a brokerage account. Still, they do not consult their partner before making trading decisions on the account. Same as what we see where lots of partners don't know what the other has saved.

This is a little sensitive or challenging; however, open, and honest financial communication is necessary if couples plan their retirement together. There needs to be a strategy that makes it interesting to talk about. You want to consider going on a date night to trash the issue or during a vacation. Whatever method works for you, but it needs to be done.

Couples Ignore Life Expectancy, Age, and Health Differences

For retiring couples, there are some sensitive topics that many ignore during retirement planning. Issues like life expectancy, age, and health are often left out. The chances are high that one partner will live longer than the other or enjoy better health; you need to plan for these.

How would the age difference impact your planning? A partner may have to start saving earlier than the other or even save more for retirement than the other. The age difference recognition will lead to a different approach in investments.

Also, one couple is younger, enjoys better health, and is more likely to live longer; it may make sense to buy a deferred income annuity in an IRA account of the younger partner. Health differences may also mean the need for long-term health care, your choice of health plans and activities signed up for during retirement.

Couples Ignore the Financial Literacy of the Other

Often, we have one spouse as the primary decision-maker when it comes to family finance. The other partner who is not up to par mostly looks away and trusts the judgment of the other. Sometimes, they are not comfortable asking many questions or lack the skillset to evaluate investment options or complex financial transactions.

The big challenge here is how the partner who is not literate enough would handle finances when the other partner dies. Will they appoint a fiduciary or trust random people with their finances? This type of weakness leaves room for fraud to take place. How does this partner handle a pressure call, sensitive information, and scare tactics from fraudulent people?

Partners should always carry each other along in decisions. In the situation where financial literacy is broad, couples must have an honest conversation about who they can trust when the decision-maker passes on.

Partners Start Social Security Without a Proper Long-Term Plan

This is another mistake common with couples when they are planning for retirement. It also has its root in poor communication. To get the most out of your Social Security, it's always better to talk to an expert.

Social Security benefits have an integrated kind of life insurance meant for married couples known as a survivor benefit. With just a little planning, you can typically get more significant benefits from the individual who made the maximum income. That greater benefit amount will last for the life span of their longest-lived spouse.

Often, a lower-earning partner can gather a spousal benefit for a couple of years while awaiting the higher earner's benefit amount to start.

Due to all of the choices available, before making a decision, married couples will need to check how their Social Security benefit option affects the other and how it impacts the family as a whole. It requires communication and working together as a unit to attain a better result.

Couples Don't Take Note of their Unique Marital Situation

A good number of couples are in at least a second marriage. This creates a unique situation that couples neglect to deal with during retirement planning. What happens if a child or children from one of these relationships are needier than others?

The challenges from these unique situations often become complicated where you have a blended family; their needs may derail your retirement planning. While it is essential to be responsible, one must be careful to ensure that their needs are checked. Additionally, couples should avoid co-signing loans for children or family members as they approach their retirement years.

Who gets what after death is another complex situation couples often shy away from. Conflicts often arise between providing for surviving spouses and making provisions for children from previous relationships.

Couples Don't Plan for All Possible Emergencies

Emergencies come in different forms; they could be health-related, leading to long-term health care or even deaths. In other cases, it could be financial/economic emergencies that can derail your financial retirement plans. For instance, Illnesses, sudden home repairs, natural disasters, and accidents can derail your financial goals.

Experts recommend having a minimum of three to 6 months worth of your household expenses accessible in cash form or simple savings accounts. Emergency funds have to be a major part of your retirement financial planning.

Couples Don't Plan to Spend Time Together

Retirement gives couples more time together than they probably planned for, leading to some underlined challenges. Before now, the most time a lot of couples spend together is perhaps the weekend or during planned vacations and in most cases with children.

However, the case is different when it comes to retirement. Couples will have more time to spend together, and they need to talk about how best to use this time. To avoid drifting apart and respecting each other's space, this needs to be an essential part of financial planning.

Couples Don't pay attention to investment taxes

Here is a common challenge couples face in their retirement planning. If you are in a high tax bracket, you need to be particularly conscious of how your resources are spent. Lots of hedge funds and mutual fund managers, for instance, don't think about taxes when they are seeking profits. Portfolio turnover could be large, and short-term capital gains, which are taxed as regular income, are usually generated in abundance.

Mutual funds can throw off what's sometimes known as "phantom income." All these are distributions of gains or capital gains that are reinvested in additional fund shares. You never really see them, but you are taxed on them all the same. Many investors wind up paying taxes on capital gains distributions even while their finance stocks have diminished in value over the years.

Couples Ignore the Effect of Inflation on their Plans

Inflation plays a pivotal role in planning for your retirement, and couples often ignore it.

Inflation is the rate at which the costs of products rise every year. It is difficult to think; but, on January 1, 1981, the U.S. inflation rate was a whopping 13.9 percent. Luckily, lately, it has been hovering between 0.5% and 2.5%. However, even today's comparatively low rate may have a detrimental impact on your buying power with time.

For instance, $2,000 now will only buy $1,000 in products 30 years from today using a 2% annual inflation rate. With the rate at 3%, that $2,000 will buy you 800 worth of products. And when inflation goes around 5 or 6%, the results might be a lot more drastic.

Higher inflation is particularly hard for most retired individuals since they might be depending on a fixed income which cannot support increasing prices. Additionally, lots of the products and services most used by retirees are already experiencing greater-than-average price inflation.

Chapter 4

Working on Your Visions for a Stress-Free Retirement

What will your lifestyle be when you finally take a bow from active work life? Will it be stressful or stress-free? Will it be a time to pursue your lifelong dreams? Living a stress-free lifestyle requires money, but that alone will not make it work. Couples need a concrete plan that takes a lot of the stress away, taking care of boredom—a plan with good and fun times with friends and family.

One of the merits of starting your financial retirement planning early as a family is to have a clearer vision for a stress-free retirement. When planning for retirement, it is crucial to anticipate the unexpected. Any range of post-retirement risk --like the earlier-than-anticipated passing of a partner, a protracted illness, stock market volatility, a broken pension program, even unplanned wellbeing --may trounce the most closely laid retirement programs.

As people live longer and in some instances are granted incentives or made to retire sooner, the probability of outliving your savings increases. The longer the retirement interval develops, the harder it might be to be sure concerning the adequacy of your resources.

Challenges That Can Derail Your Stress-Free Retirement

Below are a few of the dangers beforehand and their possible effect on your retirement financial planning. According to the [13]Society of Actuaries, some post-retirement risks may affect your income, and couples preparing for retirement or in retirement should be aware of these and prepare for them. They include;

Healthcare and Housing: Rising healthcare costs worldwide, need for long-term care, premiums, and other medical expenses.

Personal and family: unforeseen occurrences including longevity or changes in the family structure. For instance, the death of a partner or family member.

Government Policy: Changes in Medicare and Social Security

Financial: The implication of inflation, volatile stock market, variable returns on investments

Retirees face many unplanned demands for their funds and retirement plannings. So, an emergency fund needs to be a crucial part of your plans. If these demands occur during retirement when there are no backup plans, they have the potential to be harmful. The eventual consequences could lead to a drop in the money available to live a stress-free retirement and earn good returns on your investments.

Healthcare and Housing

Unplanned Medical Bills

Couples will most likely spend more on healthcare than any other item on their retirement plan. Interestingly, it is impossible to know how much you will pay, but you can work with estimates from experts and various studies. For example, according to 14HealthView Services, A 65-year-old, healthy couple can expect to spend $266,600 throughout their retirement on Medicare premiums alone. In their report, Fidelity puts their figure at $245,000. Neither of these costs includes long-term care and out-of-pocket expenses.

The need to choose the right health insurance for retirement cannot be overemphasized. Ensure you understand all the options covered for you and your spouse. For instance, find out if basic cars have a cap for out-of-pocket expenses. Also, what is the impact of comprehensive insurance on your overall plan, and can it limit your unexpected payments?

Prescription medications are a significant problem, particularly for the extremely sick. Older people typically have greater health needs and might require regular treatment for various health-related troubles. Medicare is the principal source of coverage for healthcare providers for many couples. Personal medical insurance is also accessible, but it may be expensive.

Housing

The older you get; the chances are you will need help to go about your daily activities. It's often difficult to know if the help you need will be physical help to move around or mental support. In some cases, these changes happen abruptly, because of an illness or injury, or slowly, perhaps because of chronic disease.

Retired couples might want to modify from living on their own to other kinds of housing, including assisted living or independent living in a retirement area, which provides housing. These homes are often very costly, though less pricey than nursing homes. A lot of couples wrongly believe that Medicare will help to pay for assisted living. You need to check your country's policy to know what is covered and to what extent.

Availability of Caregivers

What may be obtainable in your part of the world could be inadequate facilities or non-availability of caregivers for some particular types of illnesses, even when you can afford it. You may be unable to continue living with your spouse due to the need for a higher level of care. Understandably this may lead to emotional and financial challenges. Long-term care is a major impediment to retirees' stress-free retirement and finances.

Personal and Family

Working Risk

Deciding on the time when you need to retire is essential to retirement planning. Retiring later is a substitute for increasing your savings, but there's no certainty that proper employment will be available. Working part-time is an alternative to a full-time job, and part-time jobs might be a lot easier to find. Also, demand for employment among retirees will vary greatly because of demands for different skills and may change with health, family, or economic challenges.

Many couples intend to enhance their income by working part-time or full-time throughout retirement. In reality, some organizations might prefer to hire older employees due to their stability and lifestyle experience. Nevertheless, success in the job market might also be dependent on technical abilities that retirees can't readily gain or preserve.

Being out of a job at any point in your career will negatively impact your retirement income from Social Security and pension from employers. This may also delay you from claiming your pension if there are conditions about your years of service in your part of the world.

Early Retirement

The world is becoming more unpredictable by the day, so are the events that affect our plans. It is an open secret that unexpected events can change our carefully laid-out financial retirement plans. The average expected age stands at 66, but many people tend to retire four years earlier. According to an [15]EBRI study, Among the retirees who have to leave before their expected time, 61% retired to manage health challenges and disabilities, 18% to take care of a spouse or family members in need of special care. In all, 47% retired earlier than they had planned.

Early retirement is one of the most significant risks to couples' financial retirement plans. Imagine a scenario where you have drawn out ten to 15 years retirement plans, and then you have to stop working only eight years into the plan. Even in instances where one spouse has to continue working, it is improbable to meet your objectives.

To protect yourself against early retirement, ensure you have disability insurance to cover your income against illness or disability. Additionally, you can engage an expert to help you project what your income and expenses would look like if you were forced into early retirement. The better option would be to have incorporated this into your plan from the beginning.

Longevity

Another significant challenge for couples' financial planning is longevity and the fear of running out of funds. The [16]rise in life expectancy has increased the concerns about longevity now than ever seen. Couples should understand that the life expectancy they are working with during their retirement plan is mainly an estimate; they are likely to live longer than that.

It sounds strange to worry about not dying soon enough, but planning enough to live your life expectancy may only go halfway. The longer you live, the more likely you are to experience healthcare or long-term health challenges.

Couples in charge of managing their retirement financial planning have to carry out these balancing acts over a lifetime. If you are too cautious and spend too little, it might restrict your dream, and stress-free life, especially in the early years of your retirement. If you spend too much, you are at risk of running out of cash while you still have a long time to live.

A pension or an annuity can mitigate a few of the dangers since they can offer an income stream for life, based on the kind. However, there are a few disadvantages, such as loss of management of resources, inability to leave money for hairs, and the cost of having one.

Though it's not advisable for couples to annuitize all their assets, annuities must be considered in retirement preparation. Carefully research any company at which you would put an annuity, think about interest charges, be wary of fees, and think about different possibilities, for example, laddering bonds.

Death of a Partner

A [17]study has revealed that the terminal illness or death of a partner contributes to depression and suicide among the elderly. The death of a partner also has a financial impact on the couple's finances. It may reduce pension benefits or come with extra financial demands like debts and medical bills. The partner's death may be too much for the living spouse to handle and make them unwilling or unfit to manage the finances in the future.

Nothing derails a retirement plan more than the loss of a spouse. It has both emotional and financial effects on your retirement plans. Depending on the type of pension plans and the terms agreed to, your spouse's pension may not pay out to you in the case of your partner's death. Also, an early death will impact your Social Security, leaving the surviving partner with lesser income.

Retirement planning is not only the responsibility of the partner who earns more or the spouse who is still actively working. It is a collective duty. Hence the need for both spouses to be actively involved in the planning process to avoid sudden setbacks when a loss occurs. As weird as it may sound, plan for your death and your survivors. Consider the benefits for your surviving spouse, like life insurance. Ensure all parties are protected financially in your Will, Trust, and beneficiary designation. Where possible, create a Social Security and pension strategy that will benefit your spouse in case of any eventuality.

Survivors' pension, life insurance, and long-term care are other financial vehicles available to protect the income and needs of serving partners after the illness or death of a partner. Estate planning is another great way of providing for survivors, and couples have to plan this properly.

Marital Status

Divorce or the separation of couples living together could have significant financial challenges for both parties. It may affect benefit entitlement under private and public retirement programs and individuals' disposable earnings.

Sharing the marital assets will almost surely cause an overall reduction in living standards for the two parties, particularly when pooling resources and income created their lifestyle. Two people in their houses will require about 20% more income to keep their living standard compared to those staying at the same house. This is because some costs, such as utilities and rent, stay the same, whatever the number of individuals residing in a household.

Though divorce rates among elderly couples are much lower than younger couples, it isn't unusual for retirement-age couples to get a divorce. Prenuptial agreements might be used to specify each party's right to the house before marriage.

Consistent Support to Family Members

Many couples find their dreams of a stress-free retirement derailed by helping family members like parents, children, and even friends. The support could be due to a loss of employment, marital status, or even a decline in health conditions. This support can take the following nature;

- Paying for advanced education for children
- Financial support before and during a difficult divorce
- Financial support for medical bills and healthcare
- Support during a loss of employment

Here's another area where couples need to find a way to balance their support and the impact on their retirement planning. The continued bailing of adult kids will not only derail your plans, but it will not help the kids take responsibility for their own. Also, couples could be so deep in offering support to family members that they forget to have fun during retirement.

The way out is to set boundaries after leaving regular employment. However, if it's an issue, you can factor these expenses into your plans. After all, financial planning should recognize support for family members even if it doesn't look feasible.

Public Policy Risks

Government policies influence many facets of our lives, including the financial standing of retirees, and such policies frequently vary over time. Policy risks include potential increases in taxes or reductions in entitlement benefits from Medicare or Social Security.

Retirement planning shouldn't be predicated on the premise that government policy will remain unchanged indefinitely. It's also vital that you understand your rights and be conscious of your entitlement to state and local benefits.

Economic and Financial Risk

Interest Rate

Interest rates can consequently reduce your retirement income by reducing growth rates for savings accounts and assets. Due to this, couples may need to save more for that stress-free retirement lifestyle. Annuities would yield less income if they had low interest rates at the time of purchase.

Low returns can also reduce income for couples who depend on past investments to finance their stress-free retirement plans.

High interest rates can negatively affect the stock market and the housing market and eventually affect retirees' disposable income. Although high interest rates can be fruitful especially when they are higher than inflation, financial risks such as crashes can be harmful to interest rates and future returns. It is therefore important to plan wisely. Holding a share in a company for instance can be a way for securing long-term and safe investment. Again, hope is that the company does not go bankrupt, even though this occurs less often. That is why diversification of portfolios is critical.

Risk of Inflation

Couples who have a part of their plans on fixed income need to be worried about inflation. It can turn out to be a two-way risk because low rates of inflation may seriously impede the lifestyle of couples who live for many years. Also, unexpectedly high rates of inflation can be harmful to your fixed income.

The Society of Actuaries recommends that retirees and would-be retirees consider investing in assets that have historically grown in value during periods of inflation or those with inflation protection like [18]Treasury Inflation-Protected Securities (TIPS). Additionally, couples approaching retirement can plan to continue working full or part-time.

Stock Market Threat

Stock exchange losses can severely decrease your retirement savings. Stocks have considerably outperformed other investments over the years and are usually suggested for retirees as part of a balanced assets allocation plan or better diversification. On the other hand, the rate of return which you earn from the stock portfolio could be significantly lower than long-term trends. Stock exchange losses may severely decrease a person's retirement savings if the market value of your portfolio drops.

The series of good and poor stock returns may also affect your retirement savings, irrespective of long-term rates of yield. For instance, couples who encounter poor market yields in the first two or three years of retirement will have a different experience than another who enjoyed great market yields in the first year or two of retirement. However, the long-term return rates may be similar.

Early losses may mean less income during retirement. Later losses may have a less damaging effect, as couples might have a far shorter period over which the resources will need to survive.

Unfortunately, predicting the crash of the stock market before it happens is extremely difficult. The best approach to deal with the danger is keeping up a suitable asset allocation, especially if you're near retirement. You ought to keep a healthful allotment of your holdings in cash, bonds, real estate, and other options to stocks. Investment experts suggest that if you plan to invest in stocks as part of your asset, you may consider investing in stocks with good long-term momentum such as renewable energies, artificial intelligence, and climate.

By diversifying your shares across geographies and financial sectors, the dangers of a potential market crash are significantly reduced.

You can also protect yourself by holding up to 3 years' worth of expenditures in low-risk bonds or [19]GICs, so it is possible to ride out a fall without needing to cash in stocks. Remember, when you have enough wealth to realize your objectives with conservative investments, there is no need to take more risk than needed.

Ease into Retirement

Couples need to identify if a spouse will feel a loss of identity if they retire suddenly. This can be a significant source of stressful retirement. Your identity might have been built around your job and career such that retirement makes it look like a part of you no longer exists.

The sudden and devastating change can make you question your place in the world now that you no longer have the job. Many partners may not know this, but many people have this strong attachment to their job and career, and when it's taken away from them, it can lead to trauma.

Rather than a sudden retirement, such a partner can ease into retirement by reducing their hours at work. You can also go part-time instead of the total hours or even accept a lower role or position with lesser demands and stress. Since your identity is built around your career and the loss will crush you, why not consider consultancy or a way to pass the knowledge to a younger generation by writing a book or taking up a teaching role.

With these options, you have more time in your hands while still doing something similar to what you've always done, and you remain relevant in retirement.

The Threat of Pension Contribution

There are occasional instances where a loss of pension plans could occur, which could greatly distort your stress-free retirement plans as a couple. For example, if the employer that sponsors the pension plans goes bankrupt or the insurer becomes insolvent. Suppose you are faced with this type of challenge. In that case, there are guarantees for private pension plans under the [20]Pension Benefit Guaranty Corporation (PBGC) that may protect some of your pension income but might not cover all of it.

The fear of losing your pension plan is something couples should worry about because it happened at [21]Nortel. However, you have little to worry about, especially if you are in a public-sector benefit pension backed by taxpayers' pension. For instance, In Canada and the U.S., pension funds are protected by law, and it's unheard of for pension funds to fail.

You may confirm if you are at risk by looking at your yearly retirement figures, which will reveal a shortfall in the fund. In case you have questions, then phone up your plan administrator. But if the plan is underfunded, the company should pay up what is owed to the pensioners.

If the company is in terrible shape along with a retirement fund, there might be cause for worry. However, the risk is restricted to the extent of the shortfall. Therefore, if your retirement is 90% funded, you will lose no longer than the unfunded 10%. And if you reside in Ontario, Canada, the initial $1,000 per month is ensured by the Pension Benefits Guarantee Fund.

Make the Most of Your Free Time

One of the biggest misconceptions about retirement that couples need to overcome is that retirement is that time in your life where you should do absolutely nothing. You are expected to "eat, sleep, and repeat." This is one way to prevent depression.

Couples who enjoy stress-free retirement keep themselves engaged. The golden years of your lives are the time to do what you have always wanted. You can study more, continue working, join a support group, join organizations that help you connect with people, and keep your mind active.

[22]A study among the elderly has shown that positive social connections reduce depression. Don't allow boredom to get the best of you. Spend some days volunteering for a charity. Make your retirement deliberately stress-free by planning. Planning gives you control over what happens in most cases.

Beware of Dishonest Managers

Another primary concern for couples when thinking and planning a stress-free retirement is the fear of losing their fund to fake investment and money managers. Who can quickly forget the famous Ponzi case of Bernie Madoff? There are dishonest elements out there posing as experts and money managers who will not mind stealing from elderly retired couples.

I'm sure you have heard more than once that it's safer and better to work with an expert when planning your financial retirements. Still, it would be best if you verified the expert before trusting them. Before choosing a financial expert, ensure to check their references. Also, search the web for reviews about their work and what other clients have said about them. Check if they are members of any professional bodies, look out for previous and recent sanctions.

Beware of money managers who promise out-of-this-world returns on your investment but cannot explain in detail how they would achieve these returns. If your adviser cannot make you understand what they are selling to you, you probably should not be too fast in signing up.

Always be willing to seek a second opinion about any venture you plan to put your money into. Speak with your spouse and be on the same page about where to put your money. The more the eyes and mind, the more likely you will see if something is wrong, and vice versa. Ask questions and understand how every dime moves in and out of your portfolio. After all, it's your hard-earned money.

Couples should never use the excuse of uncertainty about the future as an excuse to avoid planning a stress-free retirement. You may not cover everything in your plan, but you will likely be depressed and end up with nothing without a plan.

Understandably, even the best retirement plans have loopholes because we can't control all the variables. However, careful planning can give us confidence in the new phase of life. Knowing and understanding the challenges ahead and factoring them into your retirement plans will provide you with more control over the circumstances and not the other way round. Have multiple plans like A, B, and C ready.

Chapter 5

Managing Your Retirement Finances - Before and After Retirement

The heartbeat or life wire of any financial retirement plan is money. Couples who are planning to enjoy the comfortable lifestyle of their dream need income from different sources. As a would-be retiree or retired couple, there are ways to generate earnings on a fixed and continuous basis.

After working for many years, would it not be nice to have your money work for you while you enjoy retirement? In many countries, you have your money built up in the Social Security or related system through your many service years and tax deductions. This is a great starting point. However, you will need to create extra diversified streams of income before and during retirement.

There are many options out there for generating retirement income, but we will only be able to explore a few here. Couples must understand each other's risk tolerance as they decide on which investment options work for them. Additionally, we are exploring ways to minimize taxes on your income.

Sources of Retirement Income

To manage your retirement income, first, you need to know where these incomes are coming from—for instance, Social Security, employer-sponsored retirement savings accounts, and the regulations governing each source. These retirement incomes have different names in different countries. However, the principles are similar.

Social Security Benefits

In the U.S., it's called Social Security, while in Canada, it is the Canadian Pensions Plan (CPP) system. A different name may apply in your country. For many couples inclusive, Social Security is a crucial source of retirement income, especially after serving your full retirement age. The significant advantage Social Security has over other sources of retirement income is the periodic adjustment for inflation.

Retirement Planning for Couples

One of the most significant decisions of your retirement planning is to decide the best time to apply for your Social Security benefits. There are options;

- You may choose to go for reduced benefits at age 62, then wait until you can claim the full benefits. Which is based on the year you were born.

- You can also decide to wait until you reach full retirement age or 70 plus to enjoy the full benefits.

Experts have always suggested that you opt for the second option because it gives you a larger payout.

For couples eligible for Social Security benefits based on work history, you may decide to draw your individual accounts together, or one partner can draw spousal benefits. If both partners have similar benefits based on work history, in that case, drawing on personal accounts will be more advantageous. However, if one person's earning is significantly larger than the other, you need to weigh your options.

If you are entitled to your benefits and spousal benefits, the Social Security Administration will pay yours first. However, Suppose your spousal benefit is higher than your retirement benefit. In that case, you will be paid a combination of benefits equaling the higher spouse's benefits.

Couples who have a minor in their relationship may be eligible for extra Social Security benefits. Check out more on Social Security in an earlier chapter.

Defined Pension Plans

If any partner has a defined retirement benefit, they should know how much pension income they would receive. These earnings are usually based on the length of time you worked in an organization, what you earned, and your age once you stopped working. As you approach retirement, you must consult your company's human resources office for all retirement eligibility questions. And once you retire, the workplace should still be an essential resource.

To begin with, you need to confirm that you are fully qualified to collect a full pension. Many private business workers become eligible after five years of working with the company, or between three and seven years.

You also need to ask the company what happens to your pension plan if you retire earlier than 65 or work beyond that age. Some businesses might reduce the amount of pension you would otherwise get if you quit working sooner or later than 65.

For married couples who are part of a defined benefit plan, your employer is legally obligated to pay some of your pension to your surviving spouse when you die. You can set the percentage at 50 or even higher. In instances where you don't want your surviving partner to get your pension, then such partner must sign a waiver relinquishing the right to the income.

Pension is a major attraction to people working in the armed forces and public services. There's a difference in the administration of public service pensions and corporate pensions.

- Government employees may be required to contribute a percentage of their after-tax earnings to their pensions.

- Government employees and military service members may be able to receive their pensions after a set time—such as 20 or 30 years—no matter how old they are or how close they are to the more traditional retirement age of 65.

- Government pensions and retired military pay tend to be adjusted automatically for inflation using a cost of living index adjustment.

Many countries have bodies that protect or ensure public officers' benefits, like the Pension Benefit Guaranty Corporation (PBGC). Some call it the Pension Service Commission. The central or federal government mostly runs these organizations to protect defined benefits pensions. They also protect pensions that end due to termination of employment. You can keep track of your pension figure by consistently checking the website of your pension managers.

Defined Contribution Plans

The primary difference of a defined contribution is that your employer can contribute to the plan or allow you to contribute too. Unlike a Defined Pension Plan, your employer is not obligated to pay you any income when you cease working with the organization. Instead, what you will get depends on how much was invested, the type of pension account it was invested in, and the duration of the investment.

For instance, in the U.S., employer-sponsored retirement plans like 401(k)s, 403(b)s, and 457s are examples of defined contribution plans. Other plans that smaller businesses use are SIMPLE IRAs, SIMPLE 401(k)s, and Simplified Employee Pension (SEP) IRAs. These plans allow you to defer your current income into a retirement plan. Also, you can decide how your fund is being invested by selecting from the options offered by the plans.

Defined contribution plans vary from defined benefit plans in some respects. To begin with, many defined contribution plans provide faster, or even instantaneous, absolute rights to any contributions that the employer has produced. You are always 100% vested in your contributions and any earnings on these contributions.

One other vital attribute of defined contribution plans is that you can typically move or roll over your accumulated assets into a new employer's plan or an IRA if you change jobs. This way, you are starting with a balance to build on when you resume a new job. If you cannot move it, you may leave your account with your former employer, so it keeps growing until you retire.

Real Estate Income

Globally, owning a rental property is an excellent way that couples can generate income during retirement. It is not a complex process if you want to invest in commercial real estate. The property will need continuous maintenance, but it will return good income in time.

Rents naturally rise over time, giving you more cushions over your cost, such as a mortgage. You can comfortably pay down or refinance your mortgage and still have some spare cash for other expenses.

Real estate requires continuous funding; it is not a one-way money generator. You need money to keep maintaining the property, and this should be budgeted. Some of these costs can be unexpected, but your income flow will not be affected if you are prepared.

Here's an example of how to earn rental income from real estate:

Monthly and Annual Rental Income

This is how to earn consistent rental income in real estate with some investment. Let's assume you are buying a property in a commercially viable area. The purchase price is $350,000 with a 20% down payment requirement.

After the down payment, your mortgage will look like this, $280,000. It's the same as buying a house—the higher your down payment, the lesser the amortized balance.

You need to pay 3% interest with a 30-year amortization. Your monthly payment will be $1,410 monthly (property tax inclusive). If we multiply that by 12 months, it comes to $16,920 annually.

For this building, the expected income is $60,000 annually. However, you will need to deduct a 5% vacancy factor because we might not have a 100% rent all through the year. Someone will move in or out, and there might be delays in getting another occupant, hence the 5% factor. That brings your income down to $57,000.

After that, you have to deduct, let's say, 35% as expenses for property management, insurance, repairs, taxes, administrative cost, and others. 35% from $57,000 will bring your income down to $37,050. This figure is called Net Operating Income, in finance. If you go ahead and deduct your annual mortgage from your Net Operating Income, you should have $20,130 left.

Let's put all this in a simple form;

The Price of the Property $350,000

Deduct: 20% Down Payment $70,000

Equals: Mortgage @3% P.A $280,000 ($16,920)

Expected Income from Rent: $60,000

Deduct: 5% Vacancy Factor $3,000

Balance: $57,000

Deduct: 35% Property Expense $19,950

Net Operating Income: $37,050

Deduct: Annual Mortgage $16,920

Your annual rental income will be $20,130

If you divide $20,130 by 12 months, you will arrive at around $1,678 per month. The purpose of showing the hypothetical example is to make you understand the process.

Still, in the above example, the likely challenge you will encounter is how to raise the down payment. You can cash out a part of your retirement savings or defined contribution to achieve this. Alternatively, You can use a home equity line of credit.

Also, if you are new to the real estate business, you can engage the service of a financial advisor or a real estate agent to work out all the details for you.

Home Equity Line of Credit (HELOC)

You may choose to use a line of credit in which the property covers the payments for the line of credit. Let's say you get a loan of $100,000 from your line of credit, then the property you bought will generate the monthly revenue on such a line of charge.

Therefore, if you borrowed $100,000 at 5% interest, amortized over 30 years, your payment is $602 per month or $7,224 annually. Bear in mind, the rental income cash flow is $20,130 per year, so if you pay $7,224 annually for your home equity credit line, you're left with $12,906 annually.

Annual Rent Income $20,130

Deduct: Annual Line of Credit $7,224

Net Annual Rent Income 12,906

Understanding the process is very important because once you do, you can apply it to the amount you can afford and continue to enjoy continuous rental income. You may even choose to refinance and pay up your mortgage earlier.

Home Equity

For couples who built their home, or have it fully paid for, you have some options to use your home to generate retirement income. You either sell it or obtain a reverse mortgage.

If you decide to sell your fully paid or self-built property, the plan is to use part of the proceeds to fund your retirement lifestyle. In most countries, the value of a property is always appreciating in value. So, if the value of your property has gone up considerably, you can sell and enjoy tax relief (The Taxpayer Relief Act of 1997) of up to $500,000 for married couples.

If you don't have a second home where you live, you need to decide if you are going for another home that costs less and pays outrightly or obtains a mortgage for your new home. Paying outrightly gives you peace of mind, but you will have less disposable income for retirement. If you decide to go for a mortgage, it means you will be saddled with the responsibility of monthly debt. In that case, the sales proceeds must be put to good use to generate the monthly mortgage and more.

Home-Flipping

Another option open to couples to earn real estate income is to engage in home-flipping. This method has become popular in recent years. Home-flipping requires some level of expertise in the real estate business. It's more than just being a landlord and collecting periodic rental income.

Home-flippers look for undervalued properties, clean them up, renovate and turn them around into lucrative and eye-catching property, then charge market value for the property. The profit is the difference between the cost of renovating the house and the sales price. Home-flippers realize profit faster than typical landlords because they only hold these properties for a few months. The yield is usually more than your regular rent.

The challenge with home-flipping is recruiting the right experts and managing them to fix the properties intended for sale. You need to ensure they stay on budget, so you do not spend more than intended and end up with a loss or lesser profit. Also, as a home flipper, you will always be in search of the next big deal.

Income from REITs

Unlike the previous instances, Real Estate Investment Trust (REIT) is another great option to enjoy passive income from real estate. With some funds, you can buy shares and own stock and enjoy dividends in return.

Here are some merits of REITs over traditional real estate investment, which makes it easier and attractive;

- You need a lesser amount to buy shares in REITs than the formal landlord process.

- Your physical presence is not required, and the trouble of managing property is off you.

- REITs shares can be sold anytime in the market to recover your fund.

- REITs can give you attractive long-term returns on your investment. (An average of 12% from 1998 to 2018)

- You can diversify across many properties or real estate sectors

- You can enjoy monthly, quarterly, and annual dividend income from your REITs investments.

The downside of REITs is the same fluctuations that affect the entire stock market where we see the rise, fall, and in some instances, crashes of the market. In these cases, the shares of REITs may equally follow the trend in the market. Long-term

REITs investors will tell you that this is not a big problem because they have seen it all.

Investing in REITs is usually the best way for beginners in real estate who don't have plenty of cash.

Online Real Estate Platforms

Another means of earning real estate income open to couples during retirement is the online real estate platforms like [23]Fundrise and [24]Crowdstreet. These platforms serve as a link between the investors and developers. Investors can invest in viable real estate projects with attractive returns. The arrangement is similar to what you have in crowdfunding.

The advantage here is investors who don't have huge capital have the opportunity to be part of a lucrative real estate deal with their little funds. Investors may participate in debt investments or equity investments, depending on the specific deal terms. These investments pay cash distributions and often offer potential returns bigger than regular returns. It also serves as a means of diversifying your portfolio.

Dividend Income

Dividend stocks offer two possible merits over bonds. To begin with, they frequently pay returns that are higher than that which bonds provide. Secondly, the best businesses increase their dividend payouts year in, year out, which means that you will enjoy an increased payout for continuing to hold your stock. Unlike bonds, in which the payout is generally fixed, the earnings flow from a dividend stock can grow over time.

Dividend stocks are often less risky than growth stocks, but it does not mean you can not lose money on them, particularly in the short term. Like most stocks, dividend stocks vary, although the better-run businesses tend to appreciate over time as they increase their payouts.

Selecting successful dividend stocks is not an easy venture; therefore, investors frequently turn to dividend stock funds, like an ETF. These funds have low-cost ratios and extend a diversified portfolio of shares so that their performance does not rely heavily on any single stock. A fund will often be less volatile than individual stocks and may grow its payout over time.

Dividend income is not the couples' preferred retirement income for nothing. It has the potential power of compounding, especially if you have a relatively healthy portfolio.

Here are two scenarios showing how dividend income works and grows.

1st Scenario

Here's a simple 20-year investment plan using the following terms;

- Starting portfolio size $1,000
- Annual Contribution $500 monthly = $6,000
- Dividend to be reinvested
- Annual Dividend Yield 2%
- Expected share price appreciation increase 1%

Using the [25]Marketbeat Dividend Calculator; your 20 Years Dividend Portfolio will look like this;

Year	Principal $	Annual Dividend $	Yield %	Yield on Cost %	Principal Increase $	Annual Contribution $	New Balance $	Cumulative Dividend $
1	1,000	20	2.00	2.02	10	6,000	7,010	20
2	7,010	142	2.02	2.05	70	6,000	13,080	162
3	13,080	267	2.04	2.08	131	6,000	19,211	428
4	19,211	396	2.06	2.11	192	6,000	25,403	824
5	25,403	529	2.08	2.15	254	6,000	31,657	1,353
6	31,657	665	2.10	2.18	317	6,000	37,974	2,018
7	37,974	806	2.12	2.21	380	6,000	44,353	2,825
8	44,353	951	2.14	2.25	444	6,000	50,797	3,776
9	50,797	1,100	2.17	2.28	508	6,000	57,305	4,876
10	57,305	1,253	2.19	2.31	573	6,000	63,878	6,129
11	63,878	1,411	2.21	2.35	639	6,000	70,517	7,541
12	70,517	1,573	2.23	2.38	705	6,000	77,222	9,114
13	77,222	1,740	2.25	2.42	772	6,000	83,994	10,854
14	83,994	1,912	2.28	2.46	840	6,000	90,834	12,766
15	90,834	2,088	2.30	2.49	908	6,000	97,742	14,854
16	97,742	2,270	2.32	2.53	977	6,000	104,720	17,124
17	104,720	2,456	2.35	2.57	1,047	6,000	111,767	19,580
18	111,767	2,647	2.37	2.61	1,118	6,000	118,885	22,227
19	118,885	2,844	2.39	2.65	1,189	6,000	126,073	25,071
20	126,073	3,046	2.42	2.69	1,261	6,000	133,334	28,117

From the table above, notice the gradual growth in the principal and dividend. Another point of notice is the incremental growth in yield on cost. **The yield on cost** (YOC) is a measure of dividend **yield** calculated by dividing a stock's current dividend by the price initially paid for that stock.

For couples retiring in 20 years who started their dividend portfolio with $1,000 and contribute $500 monthly or $6,000 annually, given all the factors above, you would have grown your portfolio to $133,334. The dividend over 20 years would be $28,117.33, an annual return of 0.51%, and an annual yield on cost of 2.69%.

2nd Scenario

Imagine the same portfolio size of $1,000 with the following changes;

- An annual contribution of $12,000
- Dividend reinvested
- Expected Annual Dividend Increase 3%
- Annual Dividend Yield 5%
- Expected Annual Share Price Appreciation 2%

Year	Principal	Annual Dividend $	Yield %	Yield on Cost %	Principal Increase $	Annual Contribution $	New Balance $	Cumulative Dividend $
1	1,000	50	5.00	5.16	20	12,000	13,020	50
2	13,020	671	5.15	5.36	260	12,000	25,280	721
3	25,280	1,341	5.30	5.58	506	12,000	37,786	2,062
4	37,786	2,064	5.46	5.80	756	12,000	50,542	4,126
5	50,542	2,844	5.63	6.04	1,011	12,000	63,553	6,970
6	63,553	3,684	5.80	6.28	1,271	12,000	76,824	10,654
7	76,824	4,587	5.97	6.54	1,536	12,000	90,360	15,241
8	90,360	5,557	6.15	6.80	1,807	12,000	104,167	20,797
9	104,167	6,598	6.33	7.08	2,083	12,000	118,251	27,395
10	118,251	7,715	6.52	7.36	2,365	12,000	132,616	35,109
11	132,616	8,911	6.72	7.66	2,652	12,000	147,268	44,021
12	147,268	10,193	6.92	7.98	2,945	12,000	162,213	54,213
13	162,213	11,564	7.13	8.30	3,244	12,000	177,458	65,777
14	177,458	13,030	7.34	8.64	3,549	12,000	193,007	78,807
15	193,007	14,597	7.56	8.99	3,860	12,000	208,867	93,404
16	208,867	16,270	7.79	9.36	4,177	12,000	225,044	109,675
17	225,044	18,056	8.02	9.74	4,501	12,000	241,545	127,731
18	241,545	19,962	8.26	10.14	4,831	12,000	258,376	147,693
19	258,376	21,993	8.51	10.55	5,168	12,000	275,544	169,686
20	275543.51	24158.36	8.77	10.98	5,511	12,000	293,054	193,845

In this case, the main difference is the higher yield and increased annual contribution from $500 monthly to $1,000. By the 20th year, your portfolio will look like the above;

- Ending balance $293,054
- Dividend income of $193,845

This is a 21.60% return on your investment and a 10.98 yield on cost.

There is a consistent growth in the portfolios because the dividend is reinvested, and the contributions are consistent. The case will not be the same if you decide to withdraw periodically or a crash in the market that affects 70% of the shares in your portfolio.

Shying away from stocks because they seem too risky is one of the biggest mistakes retiring couples can make when planning for retirement. True, the market has plenty of ups and downs, but since 1926 stocks have returned an average of about 10% a year. Bonds, CDs, bank accounts, and mattresses don't come close.

Certificates of Deposit

Investing in certificates of deposit is one of the easiest and safest investment options available to couples. A bank issues a certificate of deposit, and the FDIC usually backs them. They are generally easy to buy.

One recommended strategy for certificates of deposits is the CD ladder. This method helps you reduce the risk of putting all your funds in at a go. The ladder method allows you to set up CDs with different maturity dates. For instance, you can set up additional dates each for five years. When the one-year matures, you roll it over into a few more years and wait for the next, which is just a year away. With this strategy, you have CDs maturing every other year.

Alternatively, you could go with the barbell strategy. Here you can invest half your funds on a longer-term and the second half on a shorter term. The short-termed fund will be a near-cash form where the money is available when you need access to it.

Annuities

Annuities are a continuously popular alternative for couples planning their retirement. They offer you some advantages along with some drawbacks. Couples thinking about annuity must understand they are pretty complicated. However, there are guaranteed benefits like the monthly paycheck, which is comparatively simple.

The choices with annuities are all over the place. It is possible to structure your annuity to have an insurance-like advantage like a death benefit and pass the monthly income to a partner.

You can have the potential paycheck be predetermined, like in a fixed annuity, or make it changeable, like in a variable annuity. You can even start the payments at any future date of your choosing.

However, those choices lead not just to higher sophistication but also a higher cost. Annuity contracts are notorious because of their complex nature and hard-to-understand rules. Regardless, an annuity can offer a steady monthly income that makes retirement more fun for the perfect couple.

Bond Funds

Bond funds are an efficient means of creating a diversified portfolio of bonds without choosing many bonds yourself. A bond ETF, for instance, can give you a wide selection of a relatively narrow assortment of bonds based on the type of exposure you desire.

You can select from any typical choices like the central or federal government, corporations, states, and municipalities. Also, you can choose between short, medium, and - long-term bonds. There are also riskier issuers, for example, high-yield or junk bonds. And there are far more obscure options available.

For instance, if you would like short-term government bonds or intermediate-term company bonds, you will find a bond fund for that. If you prefer a combination of all types of bonds, then you can tow that path too. You might even concentrate on funds offering a choice of tax-free municipal bonds. The point is: you have a lot of alternatives with bond funds, and they are easier to exchange.

Bonds give steady earnings. They are usually much safer than shares and a few other market-based investments. Bond funds fall in the category of "highly recommended" for couples planning their retirement.

Equity Crowdfunding

Equity Crowdfunding and Angel investing is another source of retirement income couples may consider. Admittedly, they are high risk because, according to a [26]Forbes report, 90% of startups fail. However, you can reduce your risk or take a calculated risk by going through platforms like Wefunder, [27]AngelList, [28]SeedInvest, [29]CrowdCube, Seers, and [30]CircleUp. These platforms allow you to invest in startups offering shares in exchange for funds.

Some of these companies have turned out to be unicorns, while many others are doing very well today. The investors are happy that their risk paid good returns. Platforms like AngelList allow you to participate with as low as $1,000.

Also, you can choose to be a Syndicate Angel Investor. As part of this group, you get rare investment opportunities from the Lead syndicate, which does all the leg work of due diligence and others.

The membership fee is usually low, but you get business opportunities, not in the public space. If you want to join other investors to invest, you also determine the amount you want to invest.

Angel Syndicates are available on the platforms mentioned above and everywhere online. Just be sure to check the track record before you join.

Equity crowdfunding requires a higher level of financial literacy to participate and make the most of it. Still, once you get the hang of it, you can make a good income from them.

Income from P2P Lending

There has been an increase in online lending platforms where you can offer personal and business loans or any other purpose. Some operate in Europe or United Emirates Arabes, while others serve the U.S. Some platforms allow the participant to make loans secured by collateral, which gives the participant more confidence and reduces risk.

There are big and small players all over the place for you to choose from. Whatever the size of your capital, these platforms allow you to join other investors and lend your fund to qualified borrowers for returns. Usually taking a percentage of the profits is more safe and fruitful. Many investors who have perfected this model rake in thousands monthly and annually from P2P lending.

The list of retirement income cannot be exhausted. Some incomes are restricted to your country alone, while others are global. So, check with your investment experts before you decide on what works for you.

Ultimately, couples have to check their risk tolerance and decide on the best options for them. High-yield investments pay fast and quick returns, but they may not be suitable for you because the risk is higher. As you draw closer to retirement, you may consider safer investment options even if the returns are lower.

The Dynamics of One Partner Working While the Other is Retired

After working actively for many years, most couples can't wait to retire together and spend quality time with each other doing the things they love. However, financial and other issues can make joint retirement unattractive or challenging, especially if one partner is much older.

Consider these and many more reasons before deciding if both partners should retire at the same time.

Can You Afford Retirement at the Same Time?

According to [31]Couples and Money Study 2018 by Fidelity Investments; Some 46% of baby boomers have "no idea" of how much they need to save for retirement.

Couples need to be realistic about their retirement plans and the actual status as they approach retirement years. If one spouse started contributing late to the retirement account, this could mean they are lagging in meeting up the required income. A few extra years in the workforce can make a massive difference to how long the savings will last. If the younger spouse is a woman, there's the possibility she would live longer, and that means more years of retirement expense to pay for.

From the same Fidelity research, above 54% of couples disagree on the amount they should have saved by the time they are ready for retirement. Many couples have not taken a critical look at their finances and the feasibility of their retirement plans. One way to measure what you have per time is to use any of the online retirement calculators. It would make sense to use the one that applies to the country or economy where you are based. Optionally, you can sit with an expert and look at the figures objectively together.

If it is evident that you have not saved enough, it will make financial sense to have one spouse work for a few more years. The effect will be remarkable on your finances since the weight of the expenses is not resting on the inadequate retirement savings. Recent research has shown that delaying retirement for three to six months by a spouse could significantly impact retirement standard of living as saving an additional 1% income over 30 years.

Impact on Your Social Security

The decision by both spouses to retire at the same time might have a negative impact on your Social Security benefit, especially for the woman. The younger the couple when they retire, the smaller the monthly Social Security will be.

Younger women who retire at the same age as their older husbands stand to miss out on peak earning years that would have boosted their Social Security benefits. The same applies to those who took a break to have babies; the gap will hurt their benefits. This is because Social Security benefits are based on the highest-earning years. If you have lower than 35 years of income-earning years, The zeros of the non-working years will reduce your earnings.

Hence, it makes more sense for women to work a little longer and delay their Social Security for a higher payoff. The benefits even get higher for each year you postpone retirement. According to a Paper by Harvard Researcher Nicole Maestas, if a woman with lower earnings than her spouse continues working until age 70 rather than retiring early at age 62, she will erase much of the difference between her potential Social Security benefit and her husband's.

Who Will Pay for Medicare?

According to the Society for Human Resource Management, Only 19% of big companies provide retiree health coverage, down from 32% in 2008.

Medicare is vital and expensive for retirees, especially for couples. So, if both of you stopped working at the same time before 65, the responsibility would fall on you, which may have a severe impact on your retirement plans.

For instance, in the U.S., When you retire, you lose your company's health benefits. If you retire before 65, you will not be eligible for Medicare. However, if one spouse still works till 65, they will not have to get healthcare in the open market.

Discuss Role Changes

According to a [32]2017 Gallup Poll, Nearly six in 10 working Americans want to continue working part-time past retirement age; 11% want to work full time.

Beyond the financial implication of this decision, couples need to consider and discuss how their roles will change. These are emotional and psychological decisions that spouses need to weigh as part of the decision about whether to retire at the same time or if one person needs to continue working longer.

If you both retire at the same time, consider how much time you intend to spend together and how much you intend to dedicate to other interests and activities. The purpose is to communicate and clarify these things to avoid conflicts.

Also, you need to discuss roles in instances where one partner would be working eight hours plus and the other is retired. How will the non-working spouse spend their time? Will they take on extra roles in the house?

Retired couples need to consciously draw down on their retirement to make sure the money saved lasts longer than the rest of their lives. Quitting at the same time will reduce the lifespan of your retirement savings. Both spouses adding zero income to the savings and incurring regular expenses will do quick damage to whatever savings you have.

Chapter 6

Leveraging on Various Retirement Rules for Seniors

Paying Down Debts in Retirement

Every couple's dream is to get a job that pays well, take a 30-year mortgage, work for 30 to 35 years, pay off the mortgage in the process, and retire peacefully with no debt hanging on their necks. There was a time when this was a reality, but today it sounds more like a myth.

The fact is the idea or dream of retiring debt-free is fast fading among adults. It is more certain that more seniors will enter retirement with some form of debt or the other.

According to the U.S. Federal Reserve, the percentage of households headed by someone aged 65 and older who held any debt increased to 61% in 2016 from 38% in 1989, while real average debt rose to $86,797 from $29,918.

This report was further bolstered by a new report from the Transamerica Center for Retirement Studies, which states that four in 10 retirees cite "paying off debt" as a current financial priority—putting it on equal footing with "just getting by to cover basic living expenses" as a top concern for Retirement Studies. Almost 3 in 10 cite paying down credit card debt as a priority, while 17 percent focus on mortgage debt and 11 percent on some other consumer debt, such as medical bills or student loans.

Experts have always advised couples retiring to pay off their debts before reaching their golden years; the reality is that it is not feasible for many. Paying down debt while in retirement is very challenging for many couples due to the erratic nature of their fixed income.

Paying down debts during retirement is even more challenging. If couples are retiring with debts, there has to be a plan to manage the situation. Let us review some of the strategies you can include in your financial retirement plan, their pros and cons, and how they might help deal with your debt situation during retirement.

Stop Piling Up Debts

Couples are not always conscious to stop digging themselves into further debts while in retirement. The emphasis is on "consciousness." Many couples have lived the better part of their active lives going in and out of one debt because they had different sources of income; it had become a habit. That same habit led to the various debts that will follow you into retirement, but it has to be stopped.

Couples assume that their expenses will reduce when they enter into retirement. The fact is they tend to rise. Couples love to have lifestyles that cost money, like traveling and living in a dream home when they should be focusing on downsizing.

Most couples will depend primarily on a fixed income during retirement. So, it is imperative you consciously do not increase your debt burden. Live within your resources and be careful of high-interest debts like credit cards and pay down on debts carried into retirement.

Avoid Making More Mistakes

Many couples who are closer to retirement or in their early retirement suddenly realize they have not saved enough or have too much debt tend to make impulsive decisions to make up for the lost time and missed opportunity. They tend to take high-risk financial decisions like putting money in Ponzi schemes, become day traders, and investing in schemes that promise to double their returns within a few weeks.

Often these decisions are taken by one partner. Although with good intentions, it mostly ends up digging the family into further debts. As mentioned previously, the closer you get to retirement, the more careful you need to be with your funds.

When you realize you have not saved enough for your retirement, find other safer ways to make the most of your funds. You can start by delaying your retirement until you reach full retirement age. That way, you can get the maximum amount possible from social security. Just do not lose more money or enter into more debts.

Keep Working and Pay Down Your Debts

Suppose couples find that they are late in planning their retirement or fast approaching retirement with huge debt burdens hanging over them; rather than take more risk, it is better to look for means of making extra income. While this may seem like an obvious solution, many find it challenging to adopt.

The answer to extra income is in working. Working does not have to take the whole active nature of the previous years; you could be a consultant, writer, a gig worker, etc. These jobs might not be your ideal regular job, but at least you are getting extra income to keep paying your debt.

Alternatively, if you are not forced to retire, why not stay on the job a little longer to give your existing retirement savings more time to compound and grow, which would benefit your nest egg. Another advantage of working longer is you may extend the lifespan of your Medicare.

Downsize When Home Prices are Rising

Couples who own and live in their home may consider downsizing. If demand for property is high, it may be a good idea to sell and cut your cost on amenities.

Use the fund to buy a smaller home where you can predict the cost of maintenance and enjoy property tax in the future. Alternatively, you can consider moving to a cost-friendly location for retirees and with an affordable lifestyle, among other benefits.

Use the extra cash from the sale of the bigger house to knock off some debts. If you intend to pay a more considerable sum, you can reach out to your lender and see if you can negotiate some soft landing. You may never know what you will get until you ask. Optionally, you can engage the service of a financial expert to negotiate on your behalf. Just ensure you are not paying the expert all the money that could have gone into paying down your debt.

Consider Debt Consolidation

Debt consolidation involves taking a new credit in the form of a debt consolidation loan to pay off existing loans. It does come with some cost of its own. The purpose of debt consolidation loans is mainly;

- To reduce your monthly payment.
- To reduce interest paid on a loan
- To reduce the number of lenders.

This strategy can work if you have unused equity in your home. You can use it for a low- home equity loan.

The warning here is to approach this strategy by working with an expert because you need to ensure you are not digging yourself into further debts. Make sure you are getting significant rate cuts.

Reverse Mortgage Can Pay Your Debt

One other strategy couples can use to pay their debt is a reverse mortgage. A reverse mortgage is a loan for homeowners who are 62 or older and have significant home equity. You can borrow against the value of your home and receive a lump sum, line of credit, or fixed monthly payments.

A reverse mortgage is used initially to buy a home, and the homeowner is not required to make loan payments until the house is sold or when they move out.

If you can give up your homeownership, you may consider a reverse mortgage home equity for a line of credit. It makes money available to you for emergencies and mortgage payments. With a reverse mortgage, you can free yourself from monthly mortgage payments without depleting your retirement assets.

Credit Card Balance Transfer

Couples can consider transferring the balance from their high-interest paying cards to a lower one. This is one way of breaking away from high-interest credit card loans, but you may only use this method once.

Declare Bankruptcy

Our society has made bankruptcy sound like a taboo, but it is alright to wave the white flag when you reach your limit. After all, Bankruptcy laws exist for a reason. Plan to pay all your debts, do everything to pay them off; however, when you can no longer pay, speak with a bankruptcy expert and do what is expected. The sooner, the better for you and everyone involved.

Couples tend to make mistakes that typically spiral out of control by taking out home loans or spending retirement money to pay off debts that could have been discharged via bankruptcy.

In some parts of the world, your Social Security and some retirement accounts are protected assets in bankruptcy. Often, it is better to negotiate debt relief and settlement with your credit card issuer before declaring bankruptcy. Some lenders will be open to negotiating down your loan balance for a lesser amount. The downside to this is your credit score will take a negative hit. Although, at that stage of your life, your credit score will not matter very much.

Bankruptcy should not be your first option of getting out of debt. Still, if your financial situation declines to unbearable levels, you should certainly consider it.

It is noteworthy that bankruptcy will not free you from all debts. For example, student loans cannot be discharged through bankruptcy. Although, there is a hack to that. Couples in a dire situation can transfer their student loan to a credit card debt and later discharge it via bankruptcy.

Couples need to prioritize debt payments into their retirement plans when it becomes evident that they will be entering retirement with some debt burden. It is also essential to clean up and pay down all debts or reduce them as much as possible before retiring. Retiring is not the problem; the plan to pay down is the real deal.

Retirement Expenses for Couples

Couples have a common assumption and expectations that they will spend less than they were before retirement. This may be valid in some instances, but the spending is not primarily different as many assumed.

According to the [33]Consumer Expenditure Survey from the U.S. Bureau of Labour Statistics, the average retiree household led by someone 65 or older spends $50,220 per year. By comparison, the average annual spend across all families is $63,036.

Generally, some recurring expenses like payroll taxes, disability insurance, commuting expenses, and others disappear when you retire, many do not. They are replaced by new expenses that may cost more. Wherever you are in the world, there are some vital expenses the average couple incurs during retirement; we will be reviewing them here;

Housing Expenses

Housing cost includes rent, property taxes, mortgages, insurance, maintenance, and repairs. These are the most considerable costs on most couple's retirement plans. The average retiree spends $17,472 annually, or $1,456 monthly on housing expenses, making up 35% of their annual expenses. An average household in the U.S. spends $20,679 every year, or $1,723 monthly on housing, representing 33% of their yearly expenses.

According to a recent report by [34]Harvard's Joint Center for Housing Studies, 46% of homeowners between the ages of 65-79 and one in every four people aged 80+ are still paying off a mortgage. And, according to a [35]survey by American Financing, many responses are claiming they may never pay off their mortgage. By contrast, 34% of those aged 65-79 and 3% of those aged 80+ had mortgages in 1990. So, you can see that Americans today have less aversion to debt than they once had.

Paying off your mortgage and growing your equity before you retire may not be an excellent decision; however, it is one of the most strategic decisions you can take to reduce your living expenses after you have stopped receiving regular income. This will leave you with fewer expenses to spend on.

Another option is to consider downsizing your living arrangement so you can pay off mortgage debt. If you choose to go with this choice, ensure you get a reasonable estimate for your property and take note of closing costs and taxes. Avoid losing on this transaction instead of making more money and relieving yourself.

Healthcare

Healthcare includes medical services, health insurance, supplies, and services. Healthcare ranks top on the list of couples' retirement expenses. On average, $6,833 per year, or $569 per month, is spent by retiree households versus $5,193 for the average U.S. household. The more significant percentage of this cost comes from health insurance.

It is imperative to understand the type of healthcare available for seniors and retired couples in the area where you plan to retire finally. This knowledge can save you a lot of money. Worthy of note, too, is the availability and cost of long-term care. In some cases, you need a policy to access this Medicare. If you need to pay out of pocket, know what it costs and incorporate it into your plans.

Transportation

Indeed, your regular cost of commuting to work and back will no longer be there; hence, your transportation cost is expected to reduce. However, you still need to move around. These costs include gas, vehicle, car rental, leases, repairs and maintenance, and payments for public fares.

Transportation is often overlooked as not being part of the top expenses required for retired couples. The older you get with your spouse, the more unique and exclusive means of transportation you will need. The average retiree household spends $7,492 a year, or $624 monthly, versus $10,742 a year or $895 every month for the average U.S. household. Couples need to review this often and build it into their retirement plans.

Today, many seniors live in car-dependent cities and rural communities. So, shopping for the best auto insurance every year might be the best way to save money in this category. Alternatively, suppose you do not need to commute daily. In that case, you can save big on a car and insurance and rely on hailing cab services to move yourself and your partner around.

Food

Food is another category of expenses you must incur, and it includes eating out and food made at home. Retired couples spend an average of $6,599 annually, or $550 monthly on food, compared to $8,169 annually, or $681 monthly for the average U.S. household. Almost 40% of the spending for retiree households is for dining out.

Some strategies to save on this category include staying away from expensive, convenient foods and taking time to prepare healthy home-cooked meals. Also, you can get coupons for purchasing groceries, make a shopping list, and stick with it. Then take advantage of stores that offer seniors discounts on groceries.

The extra free time retired couples have during this time of their life might lead to incurring a high cost of feeding if not put to proper use. Also, retirement is a time to spend with family and friends eating out, but you must find a balance and ensure it does not dig a hole in your finances.

Utilities

Another top expense couples spend a lot on during retirement is utilities. They include electricity, access to the internet, water, phone, and others. Older households spend an average of $3,810 annually versus $4,055 for all households.

There are some methods to reduce your cost of these utilities. List out all your monthly expenses, rank them and vet them critically to see where you can make some adjustments.

Emergency Expenses

Every smart couple should make provision for emergencies in their retirement financial planning. It should not end when you stopped active service or when your kids have all grown up. An emergency fund can also mitigate against spending your retirement savings too quickly due to unavoidable sudden needs. Suppose you have an emergency fund for general expenses. In that case, you will not have to disrupt your retirement accounts every time something happens.

There are other expenses involved during retirement, but these are the primary ones you need to prepare for by including them in your financial retirement plans. As you can see, couples' retirement expenses drop but just by a little compared to non-retired households. Start getting control over your expenses as you approach retirement. If you need help, feel free to check some online resources or engage an expert to help you.

Impact of Interest Rates on Couples Financial Retirement Plans

While stocks and bonds have their ups and downs, which affect retirement income eventually, the most disturbing effect comes from returns because they can eat up future incomes derived from current investments, for a long time and ruin your retirement plans. Now that interest rates are low, it is the best time for couples to ensure their retirement plans reflect the accurate picture.

When working on your plans, ensure to use online resources to reflect and validate your assumptions. Alternatively, you can hire the service of a financial planner for a small fee. Let us examine the impact of low interest on some of your favorite retirement investment vehicles.

Impact of Rates on Stock and Bonds

The simple explanation behind investment in bonds and stock is, you invest your money today with the hope of reaping higher returns on your investment later in the future.

For bonds, the future returns come in the form of growth in interest and principal payments. While for stocks, it is in corporate earnings, leading to regular dividend payments and a rise in share price. You can sell your stocks at a high price in the future and pocket the gains from them.

In general, when returns are high, people might find future income less attractive because they choose to make money on short-term investments with higher returns. This is why stocks and bonds fall when the interest rate is high.

In contrast, when the return is low, this increases the motivation to invest today for a better future return. Interest rates have been falling since 2018, and this has been reflecting on the stocks and bond markets as we have seen increases since then.

Impact of Rates on Certificates of Deposits and Savings Accounts

Couples who rely on payouts from their high-yield savings accounts will see their yields drop due to low-interest rates. Additionally, when there's a rate cut, your certificates of deposits (CDs) take a hit. Historically, couples prefer to invest a large proportion of their funds in CDs because it has proved to be secure. Although returns on CDs have been falling over the years, the secured nature of CDs still makes them attractive to some retiring couples.

Impact of Rates on Long-Term Healthcare

Long-term care insurance gives couples a cheaper option of paying for a wide range of medical and assisted living health services. This is vital to every couple preparing for retirement because it can save you substantial money.

However, low interest rates can force insurance to hike premiums that are already on the rise. A portion of long-term care insurance cost is covered through yield on investments, and low interest is shrinking these returns.

Impact of Rates on Pension Funds

Pension funds depend on consistent, sustained growth of their assets, but a low-rate environment makes that impossible. There are lots of pension funds invested in fixed income; hence they depend on higher rates and stock returns. Low rates not only portend challenges for the fund alone but also for the retirees.

Although, not all pension funds are at risk of interest rate fluctuations. For example, pensions from private employers are not doing badly like those from the local municipalities and states. Existing pensioners might not experience disruptions in their payout, but if the rates stay low for a while longer, it would be a challenge for pensioners in the future. If interest rates remain low, pension funds will find it difficult to make up for the deficits.

The solution to the above challenges is to diversify your investment portfolio effectively and give high priority to investments with returns that do not strictly depend on interest rates. That way, you do not expose your income. Investments in real estate, shares, Exchange-Traded Fund (ETFs), or even a small business, for example, despite being impacted by market interest rates, their long-term momentum is more advantageous for retirements. Irrespective of the choices you make, you need to understand how they impact your retirement investment. While historical data is good, it should only serve as a guide. Use current and future projections to determine where to put your funds.

Chapter 7

Understand Your Taxes and Grow Your Withdrawals During Retirement

Pros and Cons of Withdrawal from Your Retirement Accounts

As we have seen in previous chapters, the lack of readiness for retirement keeps growing even more among couples today. Saving for the future and accumulating nest eggs is more complicated. Now, retirement savings are mainly dependent on defined-contribution plans. When you retire, even if you have saved enough money, it gets bumpy. Managing drawdowns on your retirement income is as vital as saving enough for retirement.

If you want your savings to last you and your spouse nearly as long as when you were in active service, then what strategies do you need to adopt?

It's important to mention that there are numerous retirement income accounts or pension accounts available in different countries. Each one has regulations and penalties that apply to withdrawals. Before you make any drawdowns, seek to know and understand the implication on your retirement accounts.

List all the sources of your retirement income that may look like this;

- Pension
- Annuity
- Taxable Investments
- Social Security
- 401(k) or Related defined contribution accounts
- Employment or Self-employment income
- Individual retirements accounts

Depending on where you are, there are undoubtedly other sources with different names and regulations. You need to work out how these income sources will generate regular cash flows for your family during retirement.

If you are working with a retirement budget, you will know what your retirement spending will be. Your needs will include medical costs, travel expenses, utilities, feeding, and others (see the previous chapter for details). When there's a need to make big purchases, such as buying a home or relocating, you may want to consider withdrawing from the big accounts such as Social Security and Pension Accounts. You need to consider the implication of each withdrawal and why to decide on one account over the other. What penalty or taxes apply?

If you intend to withdraw from Social Security when is the best time to claim your benefits? Do you need to wait until you reach full retirement age or 70? What about spousal benefits? Does it apply to your relationship status?

If you have a pension account, do you want to go for a lifetime stream of income or a lump sum withdrawal? Couples need to check the options that best fit their lifestyle and the implications of their choices.

How Much to Withdraw

The next phase is to plan your withdrawal strategy. Having funds in various accounts does not mean you can withdraw from them at any time of need. Some implications can cost you to lose some money if not well thought out.

Some retirement planning schemes and online calculators consider withdrawals relatively as fixed in nominal or inflation-adjusted terms. Inflation is the rate at which prices change within an economy. In reality, withdrawals vary in nature. For instance, when you are newly retired, you might be working part-time and withdrawing your salary. In that case, the amount you need from your retirement account will not be as much. You can even delay claiming your Social Security a little longer to allow it to grow further.

Additionally, in the U.S., for instance, there is required minimum distribution (RMDs) for retirement accounts like 401(k) and Traditional IRA Accounts and a few other retirement programs. When you reach 72, the government will determine a withdrawal method for the payments.

Suppose you have multiple retirement accounts from which you draw funds. In that case, some, like the traditional IRA or 401(k) accounts, are tax-deferred. Withdrawal from these accounts will be taxed at your highest marginal rate. For a

Roth account, you can enjoy tax-free withdrawals if you follow the rules.

The idea is to delay taxes for as long as possible and always withdraw funds from accounts with minor tax implications. If you consider the time value of money, you will agree that delaying taxes for a longer time makes financial sense.

Alternatively, it might be better to pay some of your taxes now to reduce the burden as you approach retirement. For instance, if you fall under the low tax bracket in retirement, but you are not yet 72, it might be wise to convert some of your traditional IRA funds to Roth IRA. This move will come with an immediate tax liability but remove the need to take RMDs from the account during your lifetime. If you do not require RMD during retirement, the funds will remain invested. If you do, the withdrawal will not be part of your taxable income.

Also, if you are still actively working at retirement age and in a higher tax bracket than you will be later, consider limiting your withdrawals from tax-free savings like Roth IRA. The tax implication on your fund will be lower when you earn less and your bracket drops.

The Categorized Nest Egg Strategy

The portioned nest egg approach involves setting up your nest egg in three categories. Where the first category contains cash or low-risk, short-term fixed-income investments for support couples for several years of anticipated needs during their retirement. These types of accounts are easily accessible, and the cost of withdrawal is minimal. With this category of accounts or funds, you do not have to withdraw from your stock investment prematurely during a downtrend in the market.

The second category can contain moderately risky investments that offer more growth in returns than the first category. These are high-quality fixed-income investments, moderate-risk balanced mutual funds, CDs, or dividend-paying stocks. If you need to withdraw from this category, you need a bit of calculation and strategy. To enjoy the maximum returns on your investment, your withdrawal should be as infrequent as possible.

The final category should contain growth vehicles like mutual funds and exchange-traded funds (ETFs). This category of your retirement investment portfolio is set up for growth. This is where you have investments requiring nearly zero interruptions and attract penalties and taxes when you attempt to withdraw from them before the agreed dates. This is where couples have assets designed to grow and last beyond their retirement days.

The 4% Rule of Thumb for Retirement Withdrawals

The 4% rule of thumb is a robust method couples can adopt to ensure their retirement savings last. Managing retirement savings is a balancing act. If you withdraw too much too early, you might run out of funds quickly. Also, if you withdraw too little or too late, you might not enjoy a fulfilling lifestyle. The 4% rule of thumb is a good strategy for couples to manage their retirement withdrawals.

What is the 4% Rule of Thumb?

This rule of thumb affirms that if you only withdraw 4% of your retirement savings every year, your retirement funds would run out before 30 years elapses. According to this rule, sticking with the 4% is the best way to ensure your retirement savings last.

This rule of thumb is based on a 1994 study by William Bengen, an investment management expert. He studied sustainable withdrawal rates for retirement portfolios. Brendan observed withdrawal rates for a 30-year rolling retirement period from 1926 to 1963. The test concluded that 4% is the highest initial withdrawal rate that would allow a retirement portfolio to last a full 30 years, notwithstanding the market conditions.

How the 4% Rule of Thumb Works

According to the 4% rule, if you retire with $500,000 in your portfolio, you will withdraw $20,000 in your first years. In subsequent years, you will withdraw $20,000 plus inflation. Meaning, if inflation for the second year was 3%, you will withdraw $20,600. The $600 extra makes up for inflation, ensuring you can maintain your usual standard of living.

For a better understanding of what you may withdrawal using the 4% rule, see the table below:

Retirement Planning for Couples

Year	Withdrawal Rate %	Retirement Savings $	Withdrawal Amount $
1st Year	0	500,000	20,000
2nd Year	Withdrawal Amount	Inflation	20,600
	$20,000	3%	
	For the 1st Year	In the 1st Year	
3rd Year	Withdrawal Amount	Inflation	21,218
	20,600	3%	
	For the 2nd Year	In the 2nd Year	
4th Year	Withdrawal Amount	Inflation	21,855
	21,218	3%	
	For the 3rd Year	In the 3rd Year	
5th Year	Withdrawal Amount	Inflation	22,511
	21,855	3%	
	For the 4th Year	In the 4th Year	

Maintaining your portfolio investment during retirement allows you to earn regular returns over time. Your investment growth will prevent you from running out of funds quickly. When you are unsure of the amount to withdraw without running out of cash in retirement, the 4% rule is a great option to start with.

Drawbacks of the 4% Rule

The 4% rule is quite helpful for retirement planning; however, it has some disadvantages and will not apply to some retirement scenarios. Bengen's 4% rule was based on the assumption that the retiree maintains a balanced portfolio of 50% common stocks and 50% immediate term Treasury. Another investment Management expert, Charles Schwab, suggests reducing exposure to stock in retirement in favor of a mix of bonds, stock, and cash.

Additionally, past market performance cannot be relied on to predict future results. Bengen's study assumes 10.3% stock returns, 5.2% returns on bonds, and a 3% inflation rate. A few analysts question if it was possible to have the same result every year in the future.

Furthermore, the 4% withdrawal rule assumes the retirees' expenses would be consistent yearly and only increasing due to inflation. In the real world, spending does vary from one year to another.

The 4% rule is predicated on a 30-year condition. This may not work for everyone, depending on the full retirement age and life expectancy. According to the Social Security Administration, the life expectancy for someone turning 65 in

2021 is about 20 years. That is ten years short of the 4% rule's condition.

People who are considering early retirement for various reasons may need to adjust their annual withdrawal to 3% so their money can last. There are low returns and high inflation; that means higher withdrawals under the 4% rule. This could lead to quicker depletion of retirement savings.

Retirees can break the rule and withdraw a lower amount. Bengen's 4% rule suggests doing this whenever the current withdrawal amount exceeds the first withdrawal amount by more than 25%.

Rules of Withdrawal Rate and Strategy

First, you need retirement income. Then you need to plan how much to withdraw periodically, so you don't spend down your account too fast. What is the best way to calculate and arrive at a safe withdrawal rate?

A safe withdrawal rate is an estimated amount of your retirement income you can withdraw annually while still leaving enough principal in your portfolio to last long, even if you are retiring when the economy and stock market are not performing well.

For instance, if you spend $8,000 for every $100,000 you have invested, you will arrive at an initial 4% withdrawal rule. According to traditional calculations, you can spend 4% of your investment each year and not be at risk of running out of funds.

For some couples, the 4% rule might not work for your type of lifestyle, and you may need to withdraw more than the example shown above. There are a few rules you can follow that will increase the probability of increasing your retirement income.

Following these rules might give you a 6% to 7% withdrawal rate of the value of your portfolio. That is, using the $100,000 portfolio amount, you might be able to withdraw $6,000 to $7,000 annually. If you intend to use these rules, you have to be flexible and be ready to tweak and make adjustments. If it does not go well at first, make some changes until you arrive at what works for your family.

Rule 1: Maintain the right amount of equities to fixed income, so your retirement income can keep up with inflation

Your portfolio should have a minimum equity of 50% and a maximum equity exposure of 80%. If you drop too far out of this range, you might be at risk of running out of cash. If you have too many equities, volatility in the market will scare you off at the worst time. If you have too much fixed income, your retirement income will not keep up with the inflation rate.

Keep the right proportion of equities to fixed income; that way, your retirement income will keep up with inflation.

Rule 2: Use a multi-asset class portfolio to maximize your withdrawal rate

A well-balanced portfolio contains at least an allocation for each of the following asset classes;

- Equities of both large and small-cap types (stocks or stock index funds)
- International equities
- Fixed incomes (cash, CDs, and bonds)

Every year you would rebalance this portfolio back to a target mix. Suppose you engage the services of financial experts who charge more than index funds; in that case, you may need to go for a lower withdrawal rate to cover the higher fee you are paying for the financial services.

Rule 3: Take pay cuts when the market is down

Much like the survival mood we adopt in real life, you receive a bonus in some years, and in other years, you experience pay cuts. This rule comes with the flexibility you need to survive changing market and economic conditions.

With this, you can protect your family's future income from deterioration when the market is down. The rule is triggered when your current withdrawal rate is 20% more than your initial withdrawal rate. For example, you have $100,000, and you start by withdrawing 7% or $7,000 annually.

If the market goes down for some years, and your portfolio is now valued at $82,000. The same $7,000 withdrawal will now be 8.5% on your current portfolio value. Now that your withdrawals now represent a more considerable portion of your portfolio, this rule will kick in. The rule says you have to reduce your current year's withdrawal by 10%. Using the example above, your withdrawal will go down to $6,300 from $7,000 for the year.

Rule 4: Accept a raise when the market is prosperous

This is the rule that everyone welcomes; it is the opposite of taking a "pay cut." The rule states that as long as there are favorable returns on the portfolio in the prior year, you can give yourself a raise.

This raise is computed by increasing your withdrawal in proportion to the increase in the consumer price index. For instance, if you are withdrawing $7,000 annually, the market returns a favorable result. The consumer price index went up by 3%. The following year, you can withdraw $7,210.

Keeping up with these rules requires discipline. The outcome is a stable retirement income, a stable lifestyle, and the ability to maintain purchasing power.

Before adopting a retirement income strategy and withdrawal rule, spend some time learning as much as you can about the subjects. There are resources available to help you get started. Some are free while others are paid.

Estimating Taxes in Retirement

Couples tend to get caught off guard when it comes to retirement taxes. This is either because they were not prepared for it or ignored it in their retirement financial planning.

Admittedly, different rules apply to every country. You will need to get acquainted with the tax law that applies to your unique situation. However, you will most likely continue to pay taxes in retirement. They are calculated on your income each year as you get paid. Different tax regulations apply to each type of income. Couples should have a good idea of how each income source reflects on their tax return so they can plan to minimize their taxes.

Having more funds for yourself and your spouse during retirement can significantly differentiate the standard of lifestyle you get to enjoy. One strategy to achieve that is to reduce your tax bill as much as you can.

Here are some examples under Canadian law:

Split Pension Income with Your Spouse

Suppose your spouse or common-law partner does not have a lot of work history and has limited contribution to the Canadian Pension Plan (CPP). In that case, you can save on taxes by sharing your CPP/QPP (Quebec Pension Plan) with them.

If you expect to be in a higher tax bracket than your spouse in retirement, you can reduce your tax obligation by shedding 50% of your income to your spouse. The savings on tax can be significant depending on factors like the difference in your marginal tax rates.

Use Your Extra Assets Wisely

If you have extra funds or assets that you are not putting to use at the moment, you can use them to cut down on your taxes. For instance, if you intend to bequeath assets or insurance policy for your kids or loved ones, setting up a trust fund can help reduce the tax you have to pay now.

Contribute More to Your Tax-Free Savings Account (TFSA)

There is no age limit on Tax-Free Savings Account contributions. So, you can continue contributing to this account even when you are retired. TFSA contributions are not tax-deductible. Income and returns made in the TFSA grow tax-free.

Since withdrawal from TFSA is not taxed, the income will not impact your tax bracket or marginal rate.

Contribute to Spousal Registered Retirement Savings Plan

The Canadian tax system allows you to pay lesser tax as retired couples if you each earn $50,000 annually than if one partner earns $100,000.

Make it part of your retirement plan as you draw close to exiting active work life to even out your future income by contributing to spousal RRSP. In this case, the partner with the higher income contributes to the lower spouse's RRSP.

If you contribute, you will claim it on your tax returns by reducing your taxable income for that year. The contribution would have been deposited in your partner's RRSP. The objective is to continue contributing until your expected income is the same.

Knowing how to order your withdrawals can help you save a lot on taxes

The tax implication of withdrawal from each source of income differs depending on your unique situation. Still, the general rule of thumb is to start with your least flexible income account first. For example, You can start with your Registered Retirement Income Fund (RRIF) or Life Income Fund (LIF), which both have annual minimum withdrawal requirements. It will be wise to follow with accounts that are not heavily taxed like the TFSA, which is not taxed at all, or non-registered investments, which are only partially taxed.

When you turn 71, you have to convert your RRSP to RRIF and any Locked-in Retirement Accounts (LIRAs) to a Life Annuity.

For RRIF and LIF, minimum withdrawals are calculated based on your age and some other factors. Due to these requirements, it makes sense to start with these accounts when considering retirement income and add others as required.

Paying taxes in retirement cannot be avoided. However, suppose you know the tax implication that applies to you or your spouse's situation in your country. In that case, you will be able to save big. What you earn is not as important as what you saved.

Chapter 8

Avoid the Risk of Drifting Apart After Retirement

Financial Reasons Why Couples Drift Apart

Retirement does affect couples, and if the situation is not appropriately managed, couples who have survived many challenges in their relationship might see themselves drifting apart. There are several issues associated with retirement that lead to divorce, and you could tell that retirement is a difficult transition for many spouses.

You are likely to see a rise in domestic squabbles due to more time spent together in the same space and adjustments in hobbies, routines, and household chores. Couples need to talk and walk each other through this new phase. Below are some reasons why couples drift apart and some recommendations to avoid falling into the same error.

Financial Faithfulness

Financial issues happen to be one of the top reasons why couples drift apart during retirement. Often the main contributor to the nest egg feels they have a right to dictate how the funds are disbursed without the other partner's consent. Then when the other partner becomes aware of some of the spending, they become unhappy and ready to quit the relationship even after many years of living together. These types of decisions had led to breakups and divorces.

Suppose couples have not developed the habit of being financially faithful before retirement. In that case, it is crucial to learn this habit quickly and adapt during retirement. If one person is aware of the other's expenses before they are incurred, they can check the other.

Irrespective of the volume of income that comes in, if caution is not factored into retirement spending, it tends to spiral out of control and negatively impact the couple's overall lifestyle.

While most couples have a joint where they carry out all family transactions, it may be better to keep some expenses separate. If there is a specific category of payments you would love to keep track of, it would be better to have a different account. You may choose to keep earnings separate for these types of expenses.

For instance, you can choose to have separate entertainment expenses to understand how much each person is spending. The source of funding such costs may be from the joint account or another. Couples need to understand and work with each other's expectations and set limits for spending.

Choosing the Right Location

Here's another reason couples need to work together to arrive at the best reason for the family. Many considerations come to play here, like the environments, the facilities available for the elderly, and how they fit your desired lifestyle. Crime rates, economic development, life expectancy, and other factors to consider when deciding on a place. One partner might have a sentimental attachment to a particular location, but the other does not want to live there during retirement. It is crucial to live where the infrastructure is healthy and fits your lifestyle.

Also, the choice of location might dig deep into your retirement savings. If now well worked out, you and your partner might be living in your dream location and not enjoying your desired lifestyle. Settling for a high-end area during retirement with no matching retirement income will cut short the lifespan of your savings very quickly.

Communication

Retirement gives couples more time to spend together, especially if both partners are retired. However, it can also turn out to be a lonely time where one partner or both are dealing with a lot inside. Whatever the situation is, help your partner understand what you are going through. Talk to each other and avoid wrong interpretations of the current situation.

Understandably, during the formative years of retirement, people go through many lifestyle changes that require some time to adapt. Talk more to each other about these things, the challenges, and expectations.

One partner will likely have a different lifestyle goal during retirement. That is normal as long as both parties are on the same page about the other's expectations and objectives. Ensure to communicate and agree on how to spend your retirement funds. Couples often get shocked at the changes they see in their partner during retirement. For example, one partner wants to spend time vacationing while the other wants to stay home all day.

Personality plays a significant role in financial discussions. Even for couples who are debt-free, there will always be a divide between spender and saver. It's essential to know the nature of your partner and have a conversation about it.

Partners who are natural savers are often viewed as risk-averse and cheapskates, while some are heavy spenders who go for the best things money can buy; they like to make a statement. Others enjoy shopping, and another set unconsciously ramps up debts. Yet, some are just natural investors; they prefer to delay gratification until they are self-sufficient.

Interestingly, many possess more than one of these traits, but they settle for the predominant personality with time. Partners need to recognize these habits and learn to manage them to avoid drift apart during retirement.

Who's Debt?

A partner might have some financial weaknesses that have led to some form of debt or outstanding obligations. Some of these obligations include credit card debts, school loans, gambling debts, or car loans. If one partner is debt-free and the other has baggage like these to deal with, this can lead to friction in retirement. The partner with the debt might expect to pay off their debt from the joint retirement income. In contrast, the debt-free partner might expect everyone to take care of their obligations individually.

While it may seem logical for the partner who brought the debt to find a solution, challenges like this may cause a strain in the relationship when the couples are supposed to be enjoying life together. Additionally, when a partner incurs a debt in some countries, it becomes the married couple's responsibility after marriage, and the same applies during retirement.

Legalities aside, couples need to work together to ensure they are debt-free as soon as possible and that one partner is not piling up debts secretly while they work to pay off others.

Estate Planning

Estate planning has continually remained a reluctant topic for most individuals and couples alike. If you feel hesitant to discuss this topic with your spouse, you are not alone. Even some rich and famous people have died intestate. However, suppose you die without a proper estate plan. In that case, you will be making the task of settling your affairs more complicated for your survivors. Having an estate plan has nothing to do with being famous or rich. It is essential to have a plan that states how you want your assets to be distributed when you pass on.

Estate planning goes beyond drafting a Will. It is thorough planning and accounting for all your assets and stating how they should be distributed smoothly to the people you desire to receive them. Couples need to work out their estate plan together and agree on the distribution of assets and when they want it to happen. It is essential to let other people know about any existing estate plan before any or both partners die.

Here's a strategy on how you can get started and have all your bases covered. Even if you engage the service of an expert, you will be doing it from a vantage point after going through this process.

Make a List of Your Physical Assets

Start from where you live at the moment. List out all the valuable items in your house. For example, television sets, washing machines, jewelry, cars, collectibles, the home itself, and everything in and at different locations.

For instance, this list will also contain assets you jointly own with your partner and other people. Clearly state your percentage holding and claim to all jointly owned assets. For properties jointly owned by your partner, you have to decide who should have the right to bequeath them. Alternatively, one person can buy off the other's share of the property.

There are laid down rules on how this should work. However, if it gets complicated, you can engage the service of an expert to help resolve it amicably. This is one of the benefits of starting early, you get to see all these loopholes and fix them to avoid all forms of controversies and litigations that can come up when you are gone.

The list will likely look longer than you imagined before you started. So, you do not have to finish the process in one day.

Make a List of Your Intangible Assets

The next process is to draw up a list of your non-physical assets. These are items that you own on paper or virtually entitled that are predicated on your death. The list will consist of things like Pension accounts, Insurance policies, bank accounts. Other items that may come in here are investment accounts, CDs, and all.

If there are joint investments, list them too with you your share of the investments and that of other parties involved.

Also, state the names and location of all physical documents not in your possession, contact information to the firm holding, physical and non-physical.

List Out All Your Debts

Make a list of all the people and organizations you are indebted to, including open credit cards, car loans, home equities, mortgages, and personal loans. Add to your notes the debt amount, the amount paid, agreements and contracts signed, and the contacts of individuals and companies involved.

Remember to include all your credit cards, the active and dormant ones. It is advisable to run a free credit report at least twice a year. This will help you identify credit card balances you may have forgotten.

Association Membership List

Make a separate list of all the organizations you belong to, including professional bodies. Add comments to show the year you joined, and positions held. You may be surprised to learn that some organizations have policies that cover their members and survivors.

This list should also contain charitable organizations that you support. If you would love to make some donations from your assets, it's a good time to state it clearly.

Keep Your Lists

When you feel you have completed this list, have a second look with your spouse to ensure everything has been accounted for. Make three copies of each list, send one to your estate administrator, keep one in the house where your partner is aware of like a safe, and the last one with another trusted person you and your partner agree on.

Update Your Retirement Accounts

For your retirement account with designated beneficiaries will pass directly to such individuals irrespective of your latest directives. The original instruction at the time of opening such an account takes precedence over your Will and Trust. If you need to make changes, you have to contact your previous employers or plan administrator and provide them with an updated list of beneficiaries. This is particularly important for couples who have been previously divorced and now remarried.

The same process applies to your insurance and annuities. Ensure you reach out to all insurers and have an updated version of your beneficiaries.

Appoint Transfer on Death Designation

When you bequeath an asset in a Will, they often go through probate. The same applies if you die intestate. The probate process can sometimes be expensive. However, accounts like Savings, CDs, and brokerage accounts are not supposed to be probatable if you plan.

If you have these types of accounts, you set them up or have them amended to have a Transfer on Death (TOD) instruction. These will enable the beneficiaries to receive the assets bequeathed to them without going through the probate process.

Choose An Estate Executor

Also, known as Estate Administrator, this person will be in charge of carrying out your last instruction when you die. It is crucial to choose this individual carefully and ensure that they are of a sound mind, financially knowledgeable, and have no questionable character.

The choice of an administrator does not have to be the surviving spouse because they might be too distraught to handle your death, among other reasons. Also, if you think there's going to be a conflict, you can appoint an expert or a firm to be your estate executor.

Write Your Will

By now, it should no longer be strange that everyone over the age of 18 should have a Will. It is a set of instructions on how your assets should be distributed when you die. It goes a long way to prevent confusion in the family. You can also include in your Will the appointment of a guardian for your minor children and designate someone to care for your pets. Any assets you desire to leave for your favorite charities can be included in your Will.

It does not cost a lot to write a Will. You can get a lawyer to draft something simple for you for as low as $150 and up to $1,000 or more for the complex ones. The prices depend on your geographic location and the content of the Will. Alternatively, you can draft something yourself using online services or available digital applications.

Below are some of the best online Will makers you can find;

- Best Overall: Nolo's Quicken WillMaker & Trust

- Best Value: US Legal Wills
- Best for Ease of Use: Trust & Will
- Best Comprehensive Estate Plan: Total Legal
- Best for Free: Do Your Own Will
- Best for Making Changes: Rocket Lawyer

If a third party drafted your Will, ensure you look through it again and carefully against the list you submitted. After confirmation, you need to sign the Will in the presence of 2 non-related witnesses who will also sign the document and have it notarized. Finally, ensure your spouse and a few other reliable people are aware of the existence and location of the Will in case they need to access it when the time comes.

Once your draft Will is complete, signed, witnessed, and notarized, it becomes a legally binding document, so your estate executor needs to be aware and have a copy when the time comes.

Review Your Estate Planning Regularly

It is essential to review your estate plans, and consequently, your Will regularly. You can do this, at least every two years, or when there's a significant change in your lives like marriage, birth or adoption of a child, divorce, acquisition of a new, and the loss of a major asset previously listed in the plan.

Estate Taxes

If you bequeath all your assets to your spouse, estate taxes will not apply in some countries. You can leave an unlimited amount of money and assets to your spouse tax-free. Otherwise, your estate will owe taxes if the value, including real estate, life insurance proceeds, retirement accounts, and investments, exceeds estate tax exemption.

According to the IRS, in 2016, the estate tax exemption was $5.45 million. Only the amount above this amount will be subject to tax if your estate is larger.

Set Up a Trust

Occasionally, leaving funds or assets to certain categories of beneficiaries in your Will may not achieve the objective you intended it for. When you bequeath something to a beneficiary through a Will, they get to use it as they like. However, a trust allows you to appoint a trustee to manage your money and assets according to your set out instructions.

A trust gives your control when you are incapable by allowing you to instruct your trustee to pay for your 28-year-old child's education, rather than risk handing over the fund to them to squander. Also, you can instruct your trustee to disburse a certain amount to your adult children when they are older, like 25, 35, or as you desire. Your trustee can also be saddled with the responsibility of paying for your medical bills and insurance payments if you are disabled.

Setting up a trust can save you from expensive legal interventions in your affairs while you are alive or dead. With a trust in place, you can avoid conservatorship, probate, and guardianship proceedings. A trust allows you to leave instructions for your assets to be disbursed according to your desire.

As couples settle into the reality of retirement, it becomes crucial to start estate planning. A comprehensive estate plan requires you to take account of your financial needs and ensure they are met, safeguarded, and distributed according to your wish.

Conclusion

According to feminist icon Gloria Steinem, "without leaps of imagination or dreaming, we lose the excitement of possibilities. Dreaming after all is a form of planning."

We often forget that planning is a document that gives structure to an idea. However, without a vision to set the plan in motion, there's no reason to follow through; the same applies to financial retirement planning for couples.

Couples who fail to plan for their finances during retirement will be setting themselves up for turbulent golden years. Retirement planning is an essential part of financial planning that cannot be overlooked. There is an increase in life expectancy hence the need to have a solid retirement plan to ensure additional sources of income and the management of medical emergencies. Also, to be financially independent and live a fulfilling lifestyle.

When couples plan their financial retirement, it does not mean their focus will be on finances alone. Retirement planning is a combination of financial discipline and planning by both partners. This experience from individual personal finance is fused to create something that works for the family in the long run.

Retirement financial planning helps budget income and expenses based on individual needs to project the couple's needs. For the most part, a financial retirement plan helps couples answer the question, "how do you want to spend your retirement?" If you can picture your lifestyle during retirement, you would determine your financial needs and plan accordingly.

For instance, if both partners decide to travel the world during retirement compared to staying around and volunteering to be part of a Non-Governmental Organisation. The financial plans for both options are different. This is one of the importance of retirement planning.

Another importance of having a financial retirement plan is that it reduces the activities you have to worry about when approaching retirement. The awareness that you have retirement income that will take care of your expenses will surely give anyone peace of mind. All you need to do is settle into retirement, relax, and live your life. Indeed, there will be a need for tweaking here and there, but it is better than not having a plan at all.

When couples start planning for their retirement earlier and at a younger age, you get to enjoy some items on your plan at a cheaper cost. For example, the premium on insurance policies is more affordable when the policyholder is younger and costs more for older people, especially the retired.

The best time to start planning for retirement is when you start earning. There is no need to when you get to a certain age. The earlier the plan takes off, the easier it will get as you approach retirement. Moreover, it reduces the burden on couples as they draw closer to exiting active work-life.

Many people postpone planning for retirement because they feel they have several more years to go. The closer you are to retiring, the more difficult it becomes to plan and achieve your dreams, even if you have all the money. Invest in your financial retirement planning in the early stages of your life when you still have the strength and energy to earn more and live more financially responsible.

Having a retirement plan early enough will help couples make efficient career-related and general financial decisions. For example, you will know if it is better to keep working at the current firm due to their better retirement plan, start working towards getting a job in another firm or even start your company. You will be surprised how someone who has 20 until retirement decides compared to another person just five years away.

A Plea From the Author

I hope you enjoyed the book and found it informative and useful. I will very much appreciate if you can leave a review on Amazon to show your satisfaction and support the author.

You can log into your Amazon account or go to:

amazon.com/ryp

You can alternatively scan

References

1 Social Security Administration - History of Social Security

https://www.ssa.gov/history/ottob.html

[2] Center for Retirement Research at Boston - Do Individuals Know When They Should be Saving for a Spouse?

https://crr.bc.edu/briefs/do-individuals-know-when-they-should-be-saving-for-a-spouse/

[3] Financial Reporter - A Quarter of Couples Never Discussed Retirement Income Plans

https://www.financialreporter.co.uk/later-life/a-quarter-of-couples-never-discuss-retirement-income-plans.html

[4] Fidelity Investment Study

https://www.fidelity.com/viewpoints/personal-finance/plan-for-rising-health-care-costs

[5] The Pew Charitable Trusts - The Complex Story of American Debt

https://www.fidelity.com/viewpoints/personal-finance/plan-for-rising-health-care-costs

[6] Suspicious Activity Reports on Elder Financial Exploitation: Issues and Trends

https://files.consumerfinance.gov/f/documents/cfpb_suspicious-activity-reports-elder-financial-exploitation_report.pdf

[7] Best places to Retire in 2021: The Annual Global Retirement Index

https://internationalliving.com/the-best-places-to-retire/

[8] FBI Uniform Crime Reporting (UCR) Program

https://www.fbi.gov/services/cjis/ucr

[9] Bankers Life Center for a Secure Retirement

https://www.bankerslife.com/research/

[10] Report on the Economic Well-Being of U.S. Households

https://www.federalreserve.gov/newsevents/pressreleases/other20200514a.htm

[11] Risks and Process of Retirement Survey by the Society of Actuaries

https://www.soa.org/globalassets/assets/Files/Research/Projects/research-2013-retirement-survey.pdf

[12] Transamerica Retirement Survey of Worker - Median Amount Working Adult Saved

https://www.transamericacenter.org/retirement-research/15th-annual-retirement-survey

[13] Society of Actuaries - Post Retirement Risks and Decisions

https://www.soa.org/globalassets/assets/files/resources/research-report/2017/post-retirement-risks-decisions.pdf

[14] 2019 Retirement Healthcare Report

https://hvsfinancial.com/wp-content/uploads/2020/03/2019-Health-Costs-Brief-12.12.19.pdf

[15] Employee Benefit Research Institute - 2017 Retirement Confidence Survey

https://www.aspeninstitute.org/wp-content/uploads/2017/03/EBRI-2017-retirement-confidence-survey.pdf

[16] Social Security Administration - Retirement and Survivor Benefits: Life Expectancy Calculator

https://www.ssa.gov/OACT/population/longevity.html

[17] Bereavement and Late-life Depression - Grief and its Complication on the Elderly

https://pubmed.ncbi.nlm.nih.gov/9046973/

[18] Treasury Inflation-Protected Securities(TIPS)

https://www.treasurydirect.gov/indiv/products/prod_tips_glance.htm

[19] Global Industry Classification Standard(GICS)

https://www.msci.com/gics#:~:text=GICS%20is%20a%20four%2Dtiered,to%20its%20principal%20business%20activity.

[20] Pension Benefit Guaranty Corporation(PBGC)

https://www.pbgc.gov/

[21] Nortel network Corporation

https://en.wikipedia.org/wiki/Nortel

[22] National Library of Medicine - Role of Positive and Negative Support

https://pubmed.ncbi.nlm.nih.gov/28035968/

[23] Fundrise

https://fundrise.com/

[24] Crowdstreet

https://www.crowdstreet.com/

[25] Marketbeat Dividend Calculator

https://www.marketbeat.com/dividends/calculator/

[26] Forbes Report

https://www.forbes.com/sites/neilpatel/2015/01/16/90-of-startups-will-fail-heres-what-you-need-to-know-about-the-10/

[27] AngelList

https://angel.co/

[28] SeedInvest

https://www.seedinvest.com/

[29] Crowdcube

https://www.crowdcube.com/

[30] CircleUp

https://circleup.com/

[31] 2018 Couple and Money Study

https://www.fidelity.com/bin-public/060_www_fidelity_com/documents/pr/couples-fact-sheet.pdf

[32] 2017 Gallup Poll - Work and Workplace

https://news.gallup.com/poll/1720/work-work-place.aspx

[33] Bureau of Labour Statistics - Consumer Expenditure Report

https://fas.org/sgp/crshttps://fas.org/sgp/crs/misc/R45911.pdf/misc/R45911.pdf

[34] Harvard Joint Center for Housing Studies

https://squaredawayblog.bc.edu/squared-away/more-retirees-today-have-a-mortgage/

[35] American Financing - Mortgage Lender Survey on Down Payment Preferences and more

https://www.americanfinancing.net/purchase/mortgage-down-payment-preferences

www.ingramcontent.com/pod-product-compliance
Lightning Source LLC
Chambersburg PA
CBHW072156100526
44589CB00015B/2249